THE UP

YOUR PLACE TO MEET GOD

Sarah Wilke
Publisher

Lynne M. Deming
World Editor

INTERDENOMINATIONAL
INTERNATIONAL
INTERRACIAL

77 EDITIONS
35 LANGUAGES

The Upper Room
September–December 2013
Edited by Susan Hibbins

The Upper Room © BRF 2013
The Bible Reading Fellowship
15 The Chambers, Vineyard, Abingdon OX14 3FE
Tel: 01865 319700; Fax: 01865 319701
Email: enquiries@brf.org.uk
Website: www.brf.org.uk
BRF is a Registered Charity

ISBN 978 0 85746 110 0

Acknowledgments

The New Revised Standard Version of the Bible, Anglicised Edition, copyright © 1989, 1995 by the Division of Christian Education of the National Council of the Churches of Christ in the USA. Used by permission. All rights reserved.

The Holy Bible, New International Version, copyright © 1979, 1984, 2011 by Biblica (formerly International Bible Society). Used by permission of Hodder & Stoughton Publishers, an Hachette UK company. All rights reserved. 'NIV' is a registered trademark of Biblical (formerly International Bible Society). UK trademark number 1448790.

Extracts from the Authorised Version of the Bible (The King James Bible), the rights in which are vested in the Crown, are reproduced by permission of the Crown's Patentee, Cambridge University Press.

Scriptures quoted from the Good News Bible published by The Bible Societies/HarperCollins Publishers Ltd, UK © American Bible Society 1966, 1971, 1976, 1992, used by permission.

Extracts from CEB copyright © 2011 by Common English Bible.

Printed in the UK by MWL.

The Upper Room: how to use this book

The Upper Room is ideal in helping us spend a quiet time with God each day. Each daily entry is based on a passage of scripture, and is followed by a meditation and prayer. Each person who contributes a meditation to the magazine seeks to relate their experience of God in a way that will help those who use The Upper Room every day.

Here are some guidelines to help you make best use of The Upper Room:

1. Read the passage of Scripture. It is a good idea to read it more than once, in order to have a fuller understanding of what it is about and what you can learn from it.
2. Read the meditation. How does it relate to your own experience? Can you identify with what the writer has outlined from their own experience or understanding?
3. Pray the written prayer. Think about how you can use it to relate to people you know, or situations that need your prayers today.
4. Think about the contributor who has written the meditation. Some Upper Room users include this person in their prayers for the day.
5. Meditate on the 'Thought for the Day', the 'Link2Life' and the 'Prayer Focus', perhaps using them again as the focus for prayer or direction for action.

Why is it important to have a daily quiet time? Many people will agree that it is the best way of keeping in touch every day with the God who sustains us, and who sends us out to do his will and show his love to the people we encounter each day. Meeting with God in this way reassures us of his presence with us, helps us to discern his will for us and makes us part of his worldwide family of Christian people through our prayers.

I hope that you will be encouraged as you use the magazine regularly as part of your daily devotions, and that God will richly bless you as you read his word and seek to learn more about him.

Susan Hibbins
UK Editor

In Times of/For Help with . . .

Below is a list of entries in this copy of *The Upper Room* relating to situations or emotions with which we may need help:

Advent/Christmas: Dec 1, 3, 8, 13, 15, 19, 20, 22, 24, 25, 26

Ageing: Oct 12, 19

Anger: Sept 3, 28; Nov 5, 26; Dec 9

Anxiety: Oct 29

Assurance: Sept 24

Bible reading: Sept 18, 28; Nov 14, 23; Dec 2

Change: Sept 10; Oct 19, 26

Christian community: Sept 18, 30; Oct 23, 28; Nov 1, 5, 18; Dec 11

Compassion: Sept 4, 14; Oct 6

Creation/nature: Sept 8, 27; Nov 8

Death/Grief: Dec 19

Discouragement: Sept 6; Oct 1, 10

Doubt: Oct 20, 29

Encouragement: Sept 7, 13; Oct 12; Dec 6, 29

Evangelism: Sept 15; Oct 12, 15; Nov 22, 26; Dec 21, 23

Failure: Sept 15

Family: Sept 1, 26, 29; Oct 12; Dec 28

Fear: Sept 9; Oct 8; Nov 7; Dec 18, 31

Financial concerns: Oct 8

Forgiveness: Sept 2; Nov 11, 19; Dec 12

Freedom: Nov 11

Friendship: Sept 7, Oct 5

Generosity/giving/stewardship: Sept 4; Oct 4, 5, 14; Nov 22

God's goodness/love: Sept 8, 27; Oct 6, 29; Nov 7, 25; Dec 3, 14

God's presence: Sept 9, 13, 26; Oct 1, 7, 24; Nov 2; Dec 5, 10, 24, 30

God's provision: Oct 5, 8, 13

Gratitude: Oct 22; Nov 27

Growth: Nov 17; Dec 7

Guidance: Sept 10, 17; Oct 20, 24; Dec 16

Healing/illness: Sept 3, 26; Oct 17; Nov 25; Dec 10, 30

Hope: Sept 8, 22; Dec 1, 20, 26

Hospitality: Sept 25; Oct 14, 21; Nov 12

Job issues: Sept 23

Joy: Nov 8; Dec 24

Judging: Nov 21

Living our faith: Sept 5, 14, 22, 29; Oct 6, 27; Nov 1, 3, 29; Dec 27, 28

Loneliness: Nov 12; Dec 26

Loss/tragedy: Sept 16, 20

Materialism: Nov 24

Mission/outreach: Sept 15, 25; Oct 6, 23, 31

New beginnings: Nov 7

Obedience: Sept 5, 17, 21; Oct 7

Parenting: Sept 1, 21, 24; Oct 11; Nov 9, 20, 30

Patience: Oct 23; Nov 5

Prayer: Sept 1, 7, 23; Oct 9, 17, 25, 30 Nov 5, 25; Dec 11, 14

Renewal: Sept 12, 19; Dec 6

Repentance: Sept 2, 11

Salvation: Oct 5; Nov 16, 28; Dec 16

Serving: Sept 4, 14, 29; Oct 10, 14, 31 Nov 13, 14, 21; Dec 18

Social issues: Sept 14, 23; Oct 31; Nov 14

Speaking about faith: Nov 10, 26; Dec 29

Spiritual gifts: Oct 13, 19; Nov 15, 29; Dec 4,

Spiritual practices: Sept 12, 18, 19; Oct 9, 11, 25; Nov 4, 17, 26; Dec 7, 11

Strength: Sept 3; Oct 16, 28

Tragedy: Dec 1

Trust: Sept 5, 30; Oct 2, 18, 24, 26; Nov 2, 21; Dec 8, 17, 31

Gifted Hands

'Ask, and it will be given you; search, and you will find; knock, and the door will be opened for you' (Matthew 7:7, CEB).

Since arriving at *The Upper Room* in July 2009, I've been touched beyond measure by the power of this prayer movement around the world.

Indeed, it is a self-sustaining movement: the daily meditations are written by you, our readers, and these meditations, in turn, inspire more readers to write. But the keeper of this perpetual-motion ministry is a thoughtful team of editors and theologians who bring deep insight and prayerful discernment to the process of selecting each daily meditation.

Since our founding in 1934, we have been blessed that God has provided thoughtful leadership to the editorial staff of *The Upper Room*. So, it is a joy to introduce you to Lindsay Gray, our new *Upper Room* managing editor. Lindsay is a bright young theologian with a deep commitment to prayer and to this ministry. During her college training we were delighted to have her join our staff as a copy editor for both our print and digital ministries. As Lindsay blossomed in this role and Mary Lou Redding prepared for her retirement, it was clear that the mantle of leadership could be gracefully passed to the next generation. Lindsay now leads the team that chooses what appears in each issue of *The Upper Room*. She brings to this process both a love for legacy and an eye for the future, and you, as a reader, should feel assured that this beloved devotional is in gifted hands.

Today, I ask you to lift up Lindsay Gray and the entire staff of *The Upper Room* in prayer.

Sarah Wilke
Publisher

The Editor writes...

My father left me his King James Bible when he died. It was already worn, since, as a Methodist local preacher, he had used it regularly for 40 years when he prepared services and wrote sermons. There are comments in the margins, cross-references and underlined verses he wanted to remember. Here and there within the pages are small pieces of paper on which he detailed orders of service, with hymns, prayers and readings all noted.

I have used his Bible since he died as part of my own devotions. My reading one morning included verses from Ezekiel 34, a passage in which God is depicted as the Good Shepherd. In the incomparable poetry of the King James Version I read: 'For thus saith the Lord God... As a shepherd seeketh out his flock in the day that he is among his sheep that are scattered; so will I seek out my sheep, and will deliver them out of all places where they have been scattered in the cloudy and dark day' (Ezekiel 34:11–12).

My New Testament reading was John 10:7–16, in which Jesus describes himself as the door of the sheepfold, giving his life for the sheep. When I turned over the pages, I was amazed to see one of my father's orders of service, in which he had used both readings to build his service and sermon around. I sat and thought about him, as I was now, reading the words of scripture and writing about them, thinking of God's love in our 'cloudy and dark day', and of Jesus, coming to share our lives and give his own for us on the cross.

How important it is that we pass on God's word to the next generation. As we read in Psalm 145: 'One generation shall laud your works to another, and shall declare your mighty acts' (v. 4, NRSV). My father left me his Bible partly to remember him but, more importantly, to pass on to me the treasures of scripture which he had discovered and wanted me to know in turn. Scripture is a priceless gift that we can all give to others.

Susan Hibbins
Editor of the UK edition

The Bible readings are selected with great care, and we urge you to include the suggested reading in your devotional time.

Left Out

Read Luke 10:21–24

Jesus said, 'I thank you, Father, Lord of heaven and earth, because you have hidden these things from the wise and the intelligent and have revealed them to infants.'

Luke 10:21 (NRSV)

We were a young couple with two young children, Bastian and Rayen. When Bastian learned to speak, I taught him to pray. We prayed together every evening.

One day I was surprised when my son said, 'Mummy, why don't we ask Daddy to pray with us?' I sadly recognised my failure to include my husband in our prayer time. But I was filled with joy that my young son had asked to have his father join us in daily prayer.

Since then, each day begins with our family of four joining hands with God, the fifth and integral member of our family. God, with infinite wisdom and love, placed a child in our lives to lead us. Eleven years has elapsed, and our relationship with God and our family prayer discipline still remain strong.

Prayer: *Loving God, forgive us for failing to invite those near us to be part of our relationship with you. Strengthen us in our life of prayer so that we may live out our devotion to you in all that we say and do. Amen*

Thought for the day: Who's waiting for an invitation to pray with me?

Ruth M. Santana Borquez (Los Lagos, Chile)

Sin and Debris

Read Romans 6:1–14
Create in me a clean heart, O God, and put a new and right spirit within me.
Psalm 51:10 (NRSV)

We recently experienced the outer fringes of a hurricane in our area. High winds whipped through the trees, leaving our garden filled with broken branches, sticks and leaves. For several hours I walked around picking up the storm debris and placing it in a pile by the road. Several times after I thought I had cleared a section of the garden, I would turn around or walk back over it again only to find more sticks and pine cones.

The thought occurred to me that the sin in our lives is often like the debris in our garden. It is hard to see ourselves as we really are. Sometimes we look, but we don't see, or don't want to see, what is there. We need a fresh perspective. The process of examining our lives helps us to gather up the sins we have missed.

The good news is that God helps us look at our lives with new eyes and open hearts. When we gather up our sins, mistakes and failures and give them to God, he cleans up our lives. And like the refuse collectors who faithfully gathered up what was left by the road, God takes away our sins for ever.

Prayer: *Help us, O God, to look honestly at our lives, and to bring our sin and disappointments before you. Help us to trust that you clean us up and set us on a new path. Amen*

Thought for the day: God offers to clean us of the sin in our lives.

Joey Yow (North Carolina, US)

I Can Do Anything!

Read Philippians 4:9–13

I praise you, for I am fearfully and wonderfully made. Wonderful are your works; that I know very well.

Psalm 139:14 (NRSV)

When I was a young child, a polio epidemic started in our country. I became ill and lost my ability to walk. Because I was young, I paid little attention to the fact that I was not like everyone else. But in my youth it became a problem. I sometimes thought that life was very unfair; nearly everyone else was healthy, but I was unlucky. I was miserable, of course, but at the same time I did my studies, and my health improved a little. In time, I gave birth to and reared a daughter. It was difficult—both physically and emotionally.

I lived like that for a long time—without faith and angry about my situation. But when I came to the Lord, everything changed. My physical problems did not go away, but peace entered my soul. This was not resignation; it was awareness that God had prepared something good for me.

I am happy. I realise that whatever body a person inhabits, those who abide in Christ will have the strength and mind of God. Now when I face adversity, I remember the Bible verse: 'Cast all your anxiety on him, because he cares for you' (1 Peter 5:7) and I move forward.

Prayer: *Thank you, Lord, for our bodies that serve us well and for the strength you give us each day. Amen*

Thought for the day: Leaning on Christ makes us strong.

Galina Samson (Voronezh, Russia)

2.4 Hours

Read Luke 6:33–38

Give, and it will be given to you. A good measure, pressed down, shaken together and running over, will be poured into your lap. For with the measure you use, it will be measured to you.

Luke 6:38 (NIV)

Many people are sticklers about tithing a tenth of their income, but tithing includes more than just our money. Sometimes, when it comes to time, we aren't so generous in giving to the Lord.

A tenth of our day is just under two and a half hours—2.4 to be exact. When we think of all the things we already cram into our day, it may seem impossible to give that much time to God. The good news is that our tithe of time doesn't have to be spent all at once. We can give more time at weekends, if necessary. We can do a variety of things as we tithe our time to God each day: study the Bible, pray for others, telephone someone, send an encouraging email, send a card to brighten someone's day, make a meal for an ill person, visit the housebound, bake biscuits for a neighbour, be a mentor to a young person who doesn't have both parents, take groceries to a needy family, take a depressed friend out for coffee or listen to a friend unload his problems.

Once these activities become habits, we might be surprised to find that a tenth of our day just isn't enough time to serve God.

Prayer: *Dear Lord, help us to devote time each day to serving you. Open our eyes to see where we are needed. Amen*

Thought for the day: God needs our time even more than our money.

Ruth O'Neil (Virginia, US)

PRAYER FOCUS: TO BE MORE GENEROUS WITH OUR TIME

Dare to Trust

Read Matthew 14:22–32

Fix our eyes on Jesus, faith's pioneer and perfecter. He endured the cross, ignoring the shame, for the sake of the joy that was laid out in front of him, and sat down at the right side of God's throne.

Hebrews 12:2 (CEB)

Sitting in church, I heard a prayer offered by a fellow member, a prayer of thanksgiving for a new family attending worship. Earlier, when members of the church had visited the family, they chose to open the door in welcome. Opening their door to strangers took a certain amount of risk for that family.

I thought about today's passage from Matthew where the disciples encounter Jesus walking on the water. I imagined myself in that scene, looking at the immense sea from my vantage point in the boat. Then I heard Jesus call to me as he called to Peter: 'Come on out!' I thought of Peter's faith to leave the safety of his boat to walk out to Jesus, and I wondered, what would I have done? To be sure, Peter became afraid and began to sink, but only after he trusted Jesus enough to leave his boat.

Jesus is asking us to trust him with our lives and to go where he commands us. If we look and listen with eyes of faith, we know Jesus' power will be with us wherever we go.

There are no waters deep enough to hold us back if we place our trust in the power of Christ. So let us wade into the water—no, step out on to the water—and truly follow the One who calls us.

Prayer: *Thank you, God, for loving us enough to call us to your work. May we hear your call, trusting you to help us move across the waters of life without fear. Amen*

Thought for the day: Today, when God calls, I will believe, follow and trust.

Ivelise Batista M. (Santo Domingo, Dominican Republic)

All in Perspective

Read 1 Thessalonians 5:1–18

Whatever is true, whatever is noble, whatever is right, whatever is pure, whatever is lovely, whatever is admirable—if anything is excellent or praiseworthy—think about such things.

Philippians 4:8 (NIV)

One morning while I was eating breakfast outside, I noticed something unusual about the day. As I looked to my left the sky was dark, very cloudy, and threatening rain. To my right the sun was shining, and a few fluffy white clouds were passing by—the promise of a gorgeous summer day. I started to think about the choices we have every day. We can look at the gloomy side of life, or we can focus on a positive attitude as much as possible.

Heartache, sadness and circumstances beyond our control are going to happen sometimes. We can face the challenge, do what we can to help, pray about it and then with God's help work to change our focus to positive, uplifting thoughts and actions.

Much pain and unhappiness exists throughout our world today. If we let ourselves dwell too long on this, we will become sad and bitter people. However, God created us to enjoy this life. We can thank him in return for this most wonderful gift by making the most of each and every day. Let's begin today by expressing our love for our wonderful Creator and by loving one another!

Prayer: *Thank you, dear Lord, for giving us life and for all your blessings we enjoy each and every day. Instil in us a good attitude and loving spirit so that others will see your love and grace at work in our lives. Amen*

Thought for the day: 'Rejoice always, pray continually, give thanks in all circumstances' (1 Thessalonians 5:16–18).

Terry Dilbeck Didelot (South Carolina, US)

Encouraging Others

Read Acts 11:19–26

He was a good man, full of the Holy Spirit and faith.
Acts 11:24 (NIV)

My friend had been going through a rough time. A long-distance move, unexpected health issues and financial concerns had put her under great pressure. We spoke over the telephone often; and invariably, conversation turned to discussion of her difficulties. My prayers for her never wavered, yet I felt that my prayers were left unanswered since her trials seemed to persist.

'I wish I could help somehow,' I said to her. 'My prayers don't seem to be enough.'

'Oh no!' she told me emphatically. 'You are an answer to my prayer. Each time I speak with you, I feel renewed and ready to move forward through this time in my life.'

A similar story is in Acts 11:19–26. The church sent Barnabas to the Christians at Antioch, who perhaps felt overwhelmed by their circumstances. 'He was a good man, full of the Holy Spirit and faith' and he provided them with assistance and encouragement. While I can't solve all my friend's problems, I can be a reassuring, encouraging presence for her as she moves forward in her life with God—an answer to prayer indeed.

Prayer: *Dear Lord, help us to be people filled with faith and the Holy Spirit. May we be like Barnabas, providing encouragement to our brothers and sisters in Christ. We pray in Jesus' name. Amen*

Thought for the day: Today I will reach out in kindness to someone in need.

Monica A. Andermann (New York, US)

God's Great Delight

Read Psalm 147:1–9

The Lord says, 'You are precious and honoured in my sight… Do not be afraid, for I am with you.'
Isaiah 43:4–5 (NIV)

My wife's cousin, Isabelle, lives at the top of a massive coastal dune. Over the years, despite the sandy conditions and with the help of lots of careful toil and compost, she has established a beautiful garden of flowering plants. She delights in showing people her garden and, with obvious pride, will tell you the name of each plant, where it came from and when it flowers. Some of her plants were gifts from friends; some were bought from rare-plant nurseries; many were grown from cuttings she collected throughout the country. A few were rescued from rubbish dumps! Isabelle's delight in her beloved flowers is a joy to behold.

Today's scripture reminds us that we are each like precious plants in God's garden. Our Creator, who 'determines the numbers of the stars and calls them each by name' (Psalm 147:4), knows our names and everything about us. Some of us God brought out of terrible situations; some were found in unexpected places; others he gathered from all parts of the earth. God rejoices when we bear flowers or fruit, no matter how insignificant it may seem. We are of great value to him, and he delights in us.

Prayer: *Thank you, God, for seeing something valuable in our lives and calling us to be your own. Amen*

Thought for the day: Though each of us is different, God delights in us all.

Gerald McCann (Western Cape, South Africa)

The Road Ahead

Read Romans 8:18–25

We know that all things work together for good for those who love God, who are called according to his purpose.
Romans 8:28 (NRSV)

While I was driving home on the motorway, dark clouds and intermittent rain showers surrounded me. As I approached a bridge, I could see a motorcyclist who had wisely stopped underneath to get out of the rain. I tend to notice motorcycles because my husband and I used to enjoy riding so much. When he died from cancer several years ago, I missed going on those pleasurable motorcycle rides with him. Now when I see other motorcyclists, I thank God for the wonderful memories my husband and I shared together as we enjoyed the beautiful scenery on our riding adventures.

Soon after I passed the bridge, I drove out of the rain and the road ahead was dry. I thought of that motorcyclist and how all around him it was dark and rainy, but just ahead the surrounding conditions were clear and dry. And then I thought about my own life, my husband's battle with cancer and how often I have felt afraid to believe that, no matter what the circumstances look like around me, God will provide.

While I may have to wait a little longer, my road ahead is going to be better than what I see now. God is faithful and has promised to work all things for good for those who love him.

Prayer: *Dear God, thank you for the promise of your presence through the Holy Spirit, even when our days seem dark and troublesome. Amen*

Thought for the day: God will be with us before, during and beyond the storm.

Cindy Owens (Ohio, US)

The Way Home

Read Psalm 19:1–6

In all thy ways acknowledge him, and he shall direct thy paths.
Proverbs 3:6 (KJV)

Here in the rural part of Texas, especially during the summer months when the skies are clear, I can watch the universe put on a show all night long. Over the days and months, I notice that every star and planet appears to be slowly but steadily moving in the sky—with one exception. No matter what time of night or what time of year, the North Star is always in the same position, providing a guiding light for those who have lost their way in the darkness. Even in this age of satnavs, I still find comfort in knowing that the North Star is always there to show me the way home.

Like the night sky, life constantly changes; and if we are not careful, we can easily get lost in the darkness. If we don't have something or someone on whom we can depend, we may never get where we want to go in life. Instead, we wander from one point to the next, always moving but never going anywhere. No matter how dark our life becomes, God's word is the guiding light that keeps us on the right path. We can follow God's light, and he will lead us home.

Prayer: *Dear God, when we are lost and searching, show us the right path to follow and guide us home. Amen*

Thought for the day: No matter how far we may stray, God is always with us to show us the way.

Link2Life: *If possible, go outside tonight and study the night sky, reflecting on God's guidance.*

Mark A. Carter (Texas, US)

Your Will Be Done

Read Luke 18:9–14

Do not be conformed to this world, but be transformed by the renewing of your minds, so that you may discern what is the will of God—what is good and acceptable and perfect.
Romans 12:2 (NRSV)

As I prayed the familiar lines with the congregation, 'Your kingdom come, your will be done on earth as it is in heaven', my mind was drawn to all of the crime, bigotry and violence in the world. How wonderful it would be if everyone submitted to the will of God! This time, a small voice within me asked, 'What about you?' Indignant, I thought, 'I don't do those terrible things!' I love the Lord, and pray for the end of the wickedness that is so prevalent in this world.

'What about you?' came the question again. Slowly, I realised that I, too, am a part of 'on earth'. While I have no control over the actions of others, I do have a say about my own actions. I am ashamed to admit that my will does not always conform to God's. While it does not result in crime, hatred or physical injury, my sin can make life on earth less 'heavenly' for me and for others. Now when I pray the Lord's Prayer I add, 'Your will be done on earth—especially in my life—as it is in heaven.'

Prayer: *Dear Lord, help us to be sensitive and obedient to your will as we pray, 'Our Father in heaven, hallowed be your name, your kingdom come, your will be done, on earth as it is in heaven. Give us today our daily bread. And forgive us our debts, as we also have forgiven our debtors. And lead us not into temptation, but deliver us from the evil one.'* Amen*

Thought for the day: When we submit to God's will, the earth reflects more of God.

Lisa Stackpole (Wisconsin, US)

PRAYER FOCUS: FOR REVIVAL IN THE LIVES OF CHRISTIANS
* Matthew 6:9–13 (NIV)

A Time Away

Read Matthew 26:17–45
After he had dismissed the crowds, [Jesus] went up the mountain by himself to pray.
Matthew 14:23 (NRSV)

Jesus was about to conclude his earthly ministry, and the events during this period were overwhelming him both physically and emotionally (see Matthew 26). Probably more than at any time, he needed support from his twelve disciples. Instead they continued to rely heavily on him, which only added to his burden of responsibilities.

Filled with the Holy Spirit, Christ knew all of the details of the events as they would be unfolding, every act leading to his betrayal and eventual crucifixion: 'You know that after two days the Passover is coming, and the Son of Man will be handed over to be crucified' (Matthew 26:2). Overwhelmed by these impending events, Jesus needed to be re-energised with power from God to be able to finish his vital ministry. Therefore, he took his disciples to Gethsemane so he could pray.

Similarly, we need power from God to enable us to build our faith amid the distractions of our daily lives. To do this, we can make a conscious decision to pull away from the 'crowds' of our many responsibilities in life, as Jesus did, and find some time to commune with God through reading and meditating on scripture and through prayer.

Prayer: *Dear God, help us to set aside the distractions of daily life and to draw closer to you. Amen*

Thought for the day: By spending time alone with God, I can serve others more fully.

Philip Polo (Nairobi, Kenya)

I Need Proof!

Read Exodus 4:1–9

Moses answered, 'What if they do not believe me or listen to me and say, "The Lord did not appear to you"?'

Exodus 4:1 (NIV)

A very large swarm of bees made its hive in the wall of our daughter's home. A professional team had to remove the hive and the many thousands of bees. Our grandchildren were given a small piece of honeycomb to take to school to show their classmates, to tell them about the swarm. However, our granddaughter Chloe, who is six, said, 'They won't believe me with just this! I need proof.' One of the workers told Chloe she would give them all pictures to back up their story.

Just as Chloe could use both the honeycomb and the pictures to validate this experience to her classmates, God used various signs to show his power to people through Moses. God had called Moses to bring the Israelites out of Egypt. Moses had been assured of God's presence with him, yet his several excuses showed a lack of confidence. So God gave Moses visible evidence to show the people.

Like Moses, I have often felt inadequate when God calls me to witness. Like Chloe, I have wanted proof to back up my testimony. It's not always easy to do what God wants, but our response is to believe and act in faith, trusting him through our obedience. God promises to be our strength daily through the Holy Spirit. He may not always give visible evidence, but he will never leave us or forsake us.

Prayer: *Dear Lord, forgive us when we question your call. Help us to walk in faith and obedience. Amen*

Thought for the day: When we step out in obedience, God leads the way.

Carolyn Schemahorn (Missouri, US)

PRAYER FOCUS: CHRISTIANS NEEDING ENCOURAGEMENT

Who is My Neighbour?

Read Matthew 25:31–40

Wanting to justify himself, [a lawyer] asked Jesus, 'And who is my neighbour?'
Luke 10:29 (NRSV)

In our street all the residents look out for each other. We regularly visit our next-door neighbour's home and at other times, our neighbours come over to visit with their little daughter and to check on us. It is very comforting to know others are concerned. Recently I came upon a car with a flat tyre so I stopped to help. The woman wanted to pay me, but I declined her offer. When she remarked about how nice I am, I replied, 'You should have met me before Jesus got hold of me.'

Such occurrences happen every day—people helping and being helped. Jesus told the parable of the Good Samaritan in answer to a question from one who sought to justify himself. At the end Jesus asked, 'Which of these three do you think was a neighbour to the man who fell into the hands of robbers?' (Luke 10:36, NIV). Of course, the correct answer is the one who helped, but the one in need was also a neighbour. The ones in need actually bring Christ to us so that we may minister to them by helping the 'least of these' (Matthew 25:40, 45).

We as Christians can be quick to help those in need—both the stranger and neighbour across the street—and be open as well to receive help when the Lord causes another person to come to our rescue. It's godly to let the love of God show in mutual deeds of love.

Prayer: *Dear God, thank you for sending us help and for sending us someone we can help. Amen*

Thought for the day: I can bless others by helping and by accepting help.

James A. Brunner (Arizona, US)

Failure?

Read 1 Corinthians 3:6–11

God made it grow.

1 Corinthians 3:6 (NIV)

One of my goals on a mission trip to Cambodia was to teach local mission workers to write meditations for *The Upper Room*. I began by showing them an issue that contained a meditation that I had written. Then I encouraged them, 'You can do this, too. *The Upper Room* is always looking for more writers from other countries.'

As I began to teach, my biggest problem was that English was not the students' first language. Each time I opened my mouth to begin a sentence, I had to be careful to use clear language. I explained that a good meditation uses a personal experience to connect to scripture and shares a lesson about how we can live faithfully with God. During each class, I tried everything I could think of to engage the students. I encouraged them to read scripture in their own language and use metaphors from their own culture. Throughout our time together, they listened politely but with little interaction. In the end, I felt like a failure.

The next day I returned to the mission. There, one of my students from the 'failed' session shyly handed me her writing. It was so good I wanted to cry. Through this experience, I learned that God can overcome the obstacles that make us feel like failures. Our job is just to turn up and do our best, leaving the outcome to God.

Prayer: *Dear God, we are working for you. Teach us to do our best and leave the results to you. Amen*

Thought for the day: God can turn our 'failures' into successes.

Dolly Dickinson (North Carolina, US)

Moving Closer

Read Romans 5:1–5
Draw near to God, and he will draw near to you.
James 4:8 (NRSV)

I was eating a meal with my boyfriend when I noticed that his chair was wobbling. One of the chair legs was resting in the track of the sliding door behind him. The chair was out of balance and he clearly could not remain comfortable in that position. I wondered what he would do—whether he would readjust his chair nearer to me or farther away. Finally he moved the chair leg out of the groove, closer to me.

This incident reminds me of my relationship with God when I have been stuck in uncomfortable or difficult situations, like losing a loved one or being betrayed by someone I trusted. Painful trials happen to all of us. At such times we can become angry and feel far from God, or we can draw near to him through prayer and reading his word. As we move closer, God guides us through our struggles and helps us stay in balance. The choice is up to us: will we become distant until God feels like a stranger, or will we draw near to him?

Prayer: *Dear God, help us to move ever closer to you so that we can enjoy more intimacy with you. Amen*

Thought for the day: God always wants us to come closer.

Link2Life: *Think of ways to draw closer to God in your daily life.*

Nal Sithy (Phnom Penh, Cambodia)

PRAYER FOCUS: THOSE WHO FEEL OUT OF BALANCE

A Winner!

Read 1 Samuel 17:37–50
Be still before the Lord, and wait patiently for him.
Psalm 37:7 (NRSV)

I am only nine years old, but my Christian faith is important to me. I also love to play football. I am not a very good player yet because I cannot do everything well.

One day as I practised kicking the ball, I realised that my life with God is similar to a football game. If a professional is playing, it is very difficult to get the ball away from him. He passes the ball accurately, constantly aiming for the goal and away from his opponents.

This is what God is like in my life. He knows exactly where to direct me to help me to overcome life's obstacles and reach my goal. This goal is loving obedience to God and the peace and joy that obedience brings. With God, I am a winner!

Prayer: *Dear God, we are lost without you. But when we allow you to guide us through the game of life, we will always be victorious. We pray as Jesus taught us, saying, 'Our Father which art in heaven, Hallowed be thy name. Thy kingdom come. Thy will be done in earth, as it is in heaven. Give us this day our daily bread. And forgive us our debts, as we forgive our debtors. And lead us not into temptation, but deliver us from evil: For thine is the kingdom, and the power, and the glory, for ever. Amen.'* *

Thought for the day: The One who created me loves me and leads me through life to victory.

Ignat Ilyushonok (Hrodna, Belarus)

Newborn Babes

Read Psalm 19:7–9

As newborn babes, desire the sincere milk of the word, that ye may grow thereby.
1 Peter 2:2 (KJV)

Recently our fourth child was born. Watching babies grow is amazing. Soon after birth, they begin to coo and smile. Then they gain head movement and begin rolling over. Suddenly, they begin to crawl and walk. However, immediately after being born, they are hungry. Instinctively, they cry, craving milk to satisfy their hunger. Our new little girl cries for milk throughout the day. As a result, she grows and grows. If she goes for a long period in the day without nursing, my wife becomes concerned that she may be ill. Healthy babies hunger.

In 1 Peter 2:2 we read, 'As newborn babes, desire the sincere milk of the word, that you may grow thereby.' Just as newborn babies crave milk, new believers crave the word of God. New believers have an innate hunger for the word; and through the word, they grow and become mature followers of Christ. We can be encouraged by new believers' hunger for God's word. Healthy followers of Christ hunger for the word.

Prayer: *Dear God, we pray that a hunger for your word will permeate the lives of your people. May we hunger for you and seek you wholeheartedly. We pray for new believers. Satisfy their longings with the sincere milk of your word. Amen*

Thought for the day: God's word satisfies the hungry soul.

Frankie Melton (South Carolina, US)

The Missing Link

Read John 14:15–23

Jesus answered [Judas (not Iscariot)], 'Those who love me will keep my word, and my Father will love them, and we will come to them and make our home with them.'
John 14:23 (NRSV)

As I put on my favourite necklace, I realised one of the links was missing. I had not known it was broken when I placed it in the drawer, but now the necklace was useless to me until the links were joined again.

A week earlier I had seen a small silver link on the carpet. Not knowing where it came from, I had picked it up and put it in a little dish on the windowsill. Now I could repair the necklace.

Like the broken necklace, we can become broken in our spiritual life. This brokenness can happen when any one of life's devastating losses comes our way—illness, death of a loved one, job loss, divorce. Feeling disconnected from God can happen when we have an argument with a family member or a friend, or when we have an unpleasant encounter with a colleague or even a stranger at the supermarket.

Our brokenness can be repaired through prayer, personal devotional time and meditation. We can reconnect with God through Bible study groups and community worship. God always provides a link for us if we will take advantage of it.

Prayer: *Help us, O God, to stay linked to you. Amen*

Thought for the day: We never have to live apart from God.

Charlene T. Eubank (Tennessee, US)

A Place in Heaven

Read Revelation 21:1–5
Even if my father and mother left me all alone, the Lord would take me in.
Psalm 27:10 (CEB)

When my mother was diagnosed with Stage 4 breast cancer, she was given only weeks to live. The news was devastating. Suddenly, I felt alone, sad and totally disconnected. I had no idea what would happen to me after my mother died. The emptiness would be enormous. At that moment, though, I remembered Psalm 27:10. I was comforted to remember that God is always with me.

During the 18 months that my mother endured her illness, God sustained me with the psalm quoted above. I was able to interact fully with her. When my mother breathed her last, I simply asked God to stand by me, and he gave me the strength and wisdom to carry on. As always, God was faithful, remained close and never let me falter.

Now, months after my mother's death, I continue to feel the pain of her absence. However, I am grateful to God that my mother's suffering has turned to joy and her pain has ceased. I am at peace, secure in the knowledge that both my mother and I rest in God's loving arms.

Prayer: *Loving God, when we experience loss, help us to remember that you remain with us to console and sustain us. Amen*

Thought for the day: God can turn our sorrow into joy.

Link2Life: *Telephone or send a card to a bereaved person you know.*

Georgina Mattute Henze (Federal District, Mexico)

Hesitation to Listen

Read 1 Samuel 8:1–9; 9:15–17 and 10:1

When Samuel caught sight of Saul, the Lord said to him, 'This is the man I spoke to you about; he will govern my people.'
1 Samuel 9:17 (NIV)

Samuel heard the Lord speak clearly. He didn't hesitate or question; he followed through immediately and anointed Saul as king. Samuel knew what God desired because Samuel listened.

In 1 Samuel 8, however, we read of Samuel's wicked sons who failed to walk in the ways of their father. When I read that chapter I wondered why Samuel's sons had not followed his example. I don't know. I feel sure that this godly man prayed for his family.

But I know sometimes I've felt like a failure as a parent, even though I've tried to be a good example. I've prayed for myself and for my children, asking for wisdom about how to bring them up. But still they don't always choose wisely and sometimes I feel that their mistakes are my fault.

Then I remember Samuel. His problems with his sons could have caused him to waver and doubt his ability to hear God. Instead, he continued to listen to him and to obey. I have that same choice—to let my failures, perceived or real, keep me second guessing my ability to hear God. Or, like Samuel, I can choose to listen and obey.

Prayer: *Dear Lord, sometimes, even when we seek your direction, failure comes and we question if we really heard you. Help us to listen when we feel like hesitating. Amen*

Thought for the day: We don't have to be perfect to hear God's voice.

Georgia Bruton (Florida, US)

PRAYER FOCUS: PARENTS OF PRODIGALS

Finding Hope

Read Romans 15:8–13

Hope does not disappoint us, because God's love has been poured into our hearts through the Holy Spirit that has been given to us.
Romans 5:5 (NRSV)

In a discussion group, someone asked us where we find 'ultimate happiness'. People answered the question in different ways. Some said they find ultimate happiness in the love of family and friends, others in the satisfaction of productive work. But a woman of deep faith had a unique perspective. Her job is to help parents identify appropriate educational arrangements for their children with serious emotional and behavioural problems. For her, ultimate happiness is 'finding where the hope is'.

We live in troubled times, when many people are without hope. Yet God is always present, always at work. Because of the life, ministry and sacrifice of Jesus Christ, millions of Christians throughout the world bring hope to people in need. Every kind word is a seed of hope. Every act of mercy sows hope. Every moment of teaching and learning is a path toward hope.

Even for Christians it is not always easy to 'abound in hope' (Romans 15:13) especially in circumstances of individual and global despair. But through worship, scripture and prayer we can gain the vision and strength to help others find where the hope is.

Prayer: *Gracious God, open our eyes to the needs of people near and far, and empower us as agents of your grace. Amen*

Thought for the day: Every kind word is a seed of hope.

Hayes Mizell (South Carolina, US)

A Thin Place

Read Matthew 28:16–20

Go therefore and make disciples of all nations.

Matthew 28:19 (NRSV)

St Columba landed on the island of Iona, off the west coast of Scotland, in AD563. He and his followers set up a base there, which later became a monastery, from where they carried the Christian gospel to neighbouring islands and to the mainland. Centuries later Viking raiders attacked the abbey and drove away the monks, and the monastery was abandoned.

In 1938, Revd George MacLeod, a Glasgow minister founded the Iona Community, arranging for unemployed craftspeople and clergy to begin the rebuilding and restoration of the Abbey.

Today, the Iona Community offers peace and tranquillity to visitors. Resident staff and volunteers provide accommodation, staff the various facilities and lead daily worship at the Abbey. Visitors, many of whom consider their visit as a pilgrimage, come from all over the world.

George MacLeod once described the island as a 'thin place', where one can feel close to the Lord. It is a place to meet with God, to pray, to offer ourselves to his service, and to continue in the footsteps of Columba in making disciples in our own time and place.

Prayer: *We thank you, dear Lord, for the opportunity to be in special places where we can meet with you and with each other. Amen*

Thought for the day: Jesus spent time alone with God. Do we?

Bill Findlay (Scotland, United Kingdom)

Baby Steps

Read Isaiah 40:28–31

Do not fear, for I am with you; do not be dismayed, for I am your God. I will strengthen you and help you; I will uphold you with my righteous right hand.

Isaiah 41:10 (NIV)

My one-year-old daughter recently learned to walk. Her first steps brought me overwhelming happiness. I spread my arms wide to receive her, and she joyfully bounded into my embrace. Becoming sure of her new footing took time, and she often stumbled. Every fall made me cringe, but I helped her to her feet and encouraged her to take a few more steps. As her parent, I knew the freedom walking would give her.

My journey with Christ is similar. When I first began to walk with him, I was thrilled by my new discovery. With the feeling of lightness in my heart and the excitement of moving toward Jesus, I could hardly keep from running. Upon being saved, I thought that my life would be easy, that I could move about freely as a follower of Christ and never stumble or fall again. That is not what God promises. He knows that we grow tired and slip in our faith, but he also assures us. If we continue to move toward the Lord, he will reach out a hand to steady us and will guide us back to the path laid out before us. God, like a good parent, knows the freedom that lies ahead.

Prayer: *Dear Father, please help us remember that we will fall down as we learn to walk and that you rejoice when we get back on our feet and move again toward you. Amen*

Thought for the day: Every step toward God is a step in the right direction.

Jada Pryor (Illinois, US)

The Ministry of Hospitality

Read 3 John 1–12

Share with the Lord's people who are in need. Practise hospitality.
Romans 12:13 (NIV)

I went to southern India with a mission team. We learned a few phrases in the local language and then set out in pairs to use those words with people we met. My friend and I saw a man sitting outside a house. We tried to start a conversation using our few phrases, which roughly translated, 'Hello. I am Nola, and this is John. We are trying to learn your language; we cannot speak your language properly.' The man spoke English and invited us into his home. His family prepared some food and drink for us, and he spent an hour helping us to learn different words. We were overwhelmed by the hospitality shown to us, especially as we were strangers from a different culture and religion. I wonder if I would have been so generous if someone from another country had knocked on my door.

Hospitality is sometimes undervalued, but it has been an important ministry from the first days of the church. Gaius, one of the early Christians, welcomed travelling missionaries and thereby shared in their work. Diotrephes was more interested in his own position in the church. Not only did he fail to welcome the missionaries, but he also tried to prevent others from doing so. Whose example will we follow?

Prayer: *Dear God, please help us to welcome others and to show them your love so that they can see you in our words and actions. Amen*

Thought for the day: To whom can I show hospitality this week?

Nola Passmore (Queensland, Australia)

Living in the Moment

Read 2 Corinthians 4:16–18

God has said, 'Never will I leave you; never will I forsake you.'
Hebrews 13:5 (NIV)

Our cousin's daughter shared an insight she had while watching her father and her young son eating ice-cream cones together. Her father was battling dementia, each day a bit less aware of what was happening around him. Her son was growing more aware of his surroundings and his place in the world with each passing day. Now they passed each other—her father sliding downward and her son growing upward. But for a moment they met around those two ice-cream cones; for that short time, they were both in the same moment.

Our moments are just that, moments. They don't last; they disappear and we move on. We live in the moment, and those moments keep changing.

God is with us in the moment, even in our difficult moments. Our troubles are far outweighed by the eternal glory ahead. God of our past and God of our future is there with us—in the moment.

Prayer: *Eternal God, we are grateful that you know every one of our moments. In Jesus' name we pray. Amen*

Thought for the day: Wherever this moment finds me, God is here.

Roger C. Palms (Florida, US)

Significance

Read Psalm 8:1–9

When I look at your heavens, the work of your fingers, the moon and the stars that you have established; what are human beings that you are mindful of them… Yet you have made them a little lower than God, and crowned them with glory and honour.

Psalm 8:3–5 (NIV)

A few days ago while I was driving, I saw the most beautiful sunset. I had just read Psalm 8 that morning, so it was fresh in my mind and I pulled over to watch. The sun was a vibrant orange as it sank over the horizon, painting the clouds with gorgeous shades of gold, red and purple. I spent some time praising God for this beauty, and I was reminded of the pictures recently taken by the Hubble space telescope that orbits our planet. I marvelled at the gigantic swirling clouds of colourful galaxies that are simply the work of God's fingers.

Sometimes I wonder as the psalmist did, 'What are human beings that you are mindful of them?' Looking at the vastness of our universe can make me feel quite small and insignificant. But God reassures us that we are 'crowned with glory and honour'. Throughout God's word we are assured that he loves us and that we are significant. What an honour!

Prayer: *Loving Creator, thank you for the beauty that you created and for being mindful of us. Amen*

Thought for the day: As insignificant as we may seem within our vast universe, God cares intimately for us.

Suzie Tors (California, US)

Angry with God

Read John 13:36—14:4

'Do not let your hearts be troubled. Believe in God, believe also in me.'
John 14:1 (NRSV)

When I was at university, I fell in love with a woman I wanted to marry. But it was not to be. I was so brokenhearted that I grew disillusioned and angry with God. In fact, while on a walk in the woods one day, I felt so angry with God that I picked up a tree branch and smashed it into pieces against a tree.

Though disappointed and angry with God, I continued to read my Bible. One day, I was reading the end of John 13, where Jesus foretold Peter's denial, and I thought about my own anger with God during that walk in the woods. But, remembering that chapter divisions did not exist in the original manuscripts, I read on. I suddenly understood for the first time that the very questions Peter was asking Jesus in John 13, Jesus continued to answer in John 14! Jesus had not spoken the words 'Do not let your hearts be troubled' into thin air; he was speaking directly to Peter! These words could be for me as well.

How comforting are the words of Jesus in the context of this revelation to Peter! Jesus loves us so much and is so very confident in his ability to save us that he is preparing a place for us.

Prayer: *O God, thank you for the light of your word that gives us hope, even when things seem as if they are falling apart. Amen*

Thought for the day: Though we may be angry with God, he always loves us.

Walter A. Puciata (Arizona, US)

Love and Power

Read Philippians 2:5–11

[The] power [for us who believe] is the same as the mighty strength [God] exerted when he raised Christ from the dead.

Ephesians 1:19–20 (NIV)

For days my wife and I had been looking for help for my mother, and we had met numerous warm, gracious people who seemed genuinely concerned. However, none of them could actually help us put together the resources we needed—until one social worker responded, 'Yes! I can help you.' This was the news that we had been searching for and longing to hear.

Love may inspire in us compassionate and comforting words for others, but that alone is not enough (see James 2:16). In raising Jesus from the dead, God gave us the good news that help is here, thereby showing both love for us and the power to defeat sin and death. The Lord loves us and also has the resources to bring us home, from death to eternal life. It brings together love and power. With Christ at work in us, we have both compassion and capability. The good news we bring to the world proclaims, 'Yes! We can help.' We believe that God is always at work for good and through our caring makes a difference in people's lives.

Prayer: *Dear Lord, may we experience your love and power in our own lives and happily share that gospel message with others. Amen*

Thought for the day: The risen Christ is living in us with love and power.

William H. Smith (Virginia, US)

Lesson Learned

Read Acts 2:42–47

Taking the five loaves and the two fish, [Jesus] looked up to heaven, and blessed and broke the loaves, and gave them to his disciples to set before the people; and he divided the two fish among them all.

Mark 6:41 (NRSV)

The small-group Bible study meetings held in our home were enriching our lives with both spiritual growth and fellowship. Before we realised what was happening, our group had outgrown the facilities of our home, a sure sign that the time had come to organise another group to be hosted at someone else's home.

This was very difficult for us as we had come to love each member of our group. I especially had a difficult time, as I did not want to give up any of them to another group. A while later, as I was pondering the situation, the Lord brought to my mind the scripture passage about the loaves and fish. I remembered that the loaves and fish were not multiplied until Jesus blessed and divided them. I then realised that in order to multiply and grow, it would be necessary to first bless and then divide.

As difficult as it was, it has been wonderful since that time to witness several new small groups created by simply releasing, blessing, and dividing. After all, each small group belongs to God!

Prayer: *Thank you, Lord, for all the lessons of life you teach us. Enable us to yield everything to you, that you may bless and multiply in our lives. We pray this in Jesus' name. Amen*

Thought for the day: What we release to God, he will bless and multiply.

Rebecca Seaton (Tennessee, US)

I Am With You

Read: Haggai 2:1–5

'Be strong, all you people of the land,' declares the Lord. 'and work. For I am with you,' declares the Lord Almighty.
Haggai 2:4 (NIV)

The prophet Haggai ministered to the people of Israel during the time when the temple in Jerusalem was being rebuilt. After 70 years of captivity, a remnant of people had returned from bondage to rebuild some semblance of the life they had known before their exile. The leader of the people was named Zerubbabel, and it was his job to rebuild the temple.

Soon after the rebuilding commenced, the people became discouraged. But the prophet Haggai stepped in with a timely message from the Lord, telling the people to be courageous because God was with them in what they were trying to do. The people were encouraged and the temple construction resumed.

Sometimes I feel overwhelmed by all of the problems that life brings. Economic, health and relationship issues affect just about everyone. Often pressure and stress make us wonder how we can keep moving forward.

During these times, we can find great comfort in Haggai's message, remembering that the Lord who made the heavens is always near and has promised never to leave us or forsake us. We can go to the Lord with every struggle and find peace for our souls.

Prayer: *O God, you know the problems we face. Thank you for being with us and helping us in every need. Amen*

Thought for the day: With God's help, no burden is too great.

Willard Stringham (Kansas, US)

PRAYER FOCUS: THOSE WHO FEAR THE FUTURE

Giving Up Control

Read Psalm 46:1–3

All who are led by the Spirit of God are children of God.
Romans 8:14 (NRSV)

I was struggling with one of those unfathomable issues that happen with computers. So I called the shop where I had bought it. The person who usually helped me was out, so someone I did not know came on the phone to help me.

Instead of giving detailed instructions over the phone, he used an internet program that gave him access to my computer. I sat back and watched the cursor dance across the screen, delving deep into my operating systems. Characters appeared which were being typed from the tech's keyboard.

Suddenly it struck me: without any hesitation I had trusted someone I did not know at all to take total control of my computer. When do I allow Christ, whom I know, to take total control of my life? When do any of us step back and trust the Spirit of God to lead us? How often, rather, do we resist when God wants to take over and lead us and our congregations into ministry and mission?

My spiritual needs are greater than my computer needs. I pray that the Spirit will intercede (Romans 8:26), that I may act according to God's good will. May God's will be done in me, and in all of us.

Prayer: *Spirit of Christ, take our hands, our minds and our hearts as your own, and use us to do mighty works in your name. Amen*

Thought for the day: Let us not only love God, but also trust him.

Frank Ramirez (Pennsylvania, US)

Either Way

Read Daniel 3:8–18

Shadrach, Meshach and Abednego replied to the king, 'O Nebuchadnezzar… even if [the God we serve] does not [deliver us]… we will not serve your gods or worship the image of gold you have set up.'
Daniel 3:18 (NIV)

I was overwhelmed with fear when I heard that my dad needed open-heart surgery and that there was a chance he would die on the operating table. The next day, I breathed a sigh of relief when the surgeon told us that Dad had survived the surgery. Our pastor told us something my dad had said to him the night before. Aware that he might not survive the surgery, Dad declared, 'I'll be a winner either way, no matter what happens.' My dad grew up in a Christian orphanage where he was taught that he would always have a heavenly Father who would take care of him.

Our scripture reading for today tells us that Shadrach, Meshach and Abednego knew they served a God who could save them even when they were thrown into a fiery furnace. But they also vowed, 'Even if he does not… we will not serve your gods or worship the image of gold you have set up.'

When the problems and pains of life challenge our faith, we pray that God will bring us the relief we desire. But may our faith increase so that we can declare, 'Even if God doesn't answer the way I would prefer, my faith is in my God.'

Prayer: *Dear Father, help us to trust that, whatever the outcome, you are with us through every one of life's challenges. Amen*

Thought for the day: Whether or not we get what we pray for, God loves us and is working for our good.

Brenda Tucker (South Carolina, US)

Bring Tithes

Read Malachi 3:8–12

Bring the full tithe into the storehouse, so that there may be food in my house, and thus put me to the test, says the Lord of hosts; see if I will not open the windows of heaven for you and pour down for you an overflowing blessing.

Malachi 3:10 (NRSV)

I love the book of Malachi and have underlined many of its verses in my Bible. They bring me consolation and sometimes tears. But I had not often looked at the verses about tithes. After all, that message is not for me, I thought. I give money, time and energy.

Today, when our pastor preached about tithing and what it actually means, some people lowered their eyes and looked at the floor. But for me this was a revelation. If every believer brought their tithe to the house of God along with some yearning and diligence, we could engage in many wonderful ministries. We could give daily bread to so many people and serve those whom God loves so deeply. Is this not a great joy? From now on I always want to be part of this joy.

Prayer: *Dear Lord, help us to be faithful in small things and obey your word so that we might always follow you. Amen*

Thought for the day: Today I will give joyfully to further God's work.

Liliya Teplyuk (St Petersburg, Russia)

A Perfect Gift

Read Ephesians 2:1–10

It is by grace you have been saved, through faith—and this is not from yourselves, it is the gift of God.
Ephesians 2:8 (NIV)

For my birthday, my best friend gave me two gifts: a toolbox and a pair of earrings. When I opened the gifts, I laughed at how incongruous they were and how they were so perfect for me.

Only someone who knew me well would think to give me these two presents, someone who knew that I often reached for a table knife as a substitute for a screwdriver or used my rolling pin as a hammer. She would understand, too, how much I love wearing earrings. They were perfect gifts.

Ephesians 2:8 mentions a more perfect gift: the gift of salvation. It is a free, no-strings-attached gift. A gift from God must be perfect because God is perfect.

My friend knows me and knows my needs and desires. God knows us even better than a close friend does, better, in fact, than we know ourselves. God knows us so well that, as Jesus told us, 'even the very hairs of your head are all numbered' (Matthew 10:30). God knows we need a saviour; we cannot save ourselves. He not only knows us but loves us as well. Because of love, God offers us a gift that is exactly what we need. Jesus is the perfect gift.

Prayer: *Thank you, God, for sending Jesus to be the Saviour of the world. Amen*

Thought for the day: Perfect gifts come from the loving heart of God.

Eva C. Maddox (Delaware, US)

PRAYER FOCUS: TO RECEIVE GOD'S PERFECT GIFT

To Be Like Jesus

Read 2 Corinthians 1:3–7

Be imitators of me, as I am of Christ.
1 Corinthians 11:1 (NRSV)

It was my pleasure to have known Brother Leo, a rescue mission manager. Leo was the most approachable man I have ever known. He genuinely loved outcasts. He routinely put his arms around the alcoholic's shoulders, pleading with him to surrender his life to Christ. He evoked laughter from people who had so little to be happy about. He wept with others over their shared heartaches. These men recognised that Leo cared and many responded when he witnessed to his faith.

How much Leo imitated our Lord! The woman taken in the act of adultery (see John 8:1–9) and the tree-climbing tax cheat (see Luke 19:1–6), Jesus loved them all. He was available to all, and all approached him. He was never ashamed of bad company but rather encouraged sinners to come. He worked in their lives and helped them to be transformed.

It was my pleasure to have known Brother Leo, but my greater pleasure is to know the One whom Leo patterned his life after.

Prayer: *Dear Lord, strip us of the temptation to be judgmental. Kindle in us the desire to reflect Jesus to everyone we meet. Amen*

Thought for the day: I want to be like Jesus.

Thomas Buice (Tennessee, US)

When No One is Looking

Read Philippians 2:12–18

Conduct yourselves in a manner worthy of the gospel of Christ.
Philippians 1:27 (NIV)

At the factory where I work, forklift drivers are required to wear seatbelts at all times. This is because even a minor collision can be fatal. Still, safety rules can be frustrating when you are in a hurry. I was working alone one evening, tired and eager to finish my tasks. Knowing the safety co-ordinator had already gone home, I was tempted to ignore the seatbelt policy. Who would know? But I obeyed anyway—not because I feared getting into trouble, but because it was for my own good.

Paul feared that his friends at Philippi might live differently if no one held them accountable. He acknowledged how they had obeyed him while he was with them and then explained that it was even more important that they remain obedient in his absence. I can relate to that. It is easy for me to be Christ-like when I know others are watching me. But when I am alone or with strangers, I am often tempted to compromise my values and revert to bad habits.

Just like the seatbelt policy at work, God's rules about how we should act are for our own good. When we are tempted to compromise, we can remember that each act of obedience draws us one step closer to Jesus—and he is always paying attention to us.

Prayer: *Dear God, thank you for sending Jesus to show us the way to live. Strengthen us when we are tempted to compromise our integrity. In Jesus' name. Amen*

Thought for the day: Being a follower of Jesus is a full-time job.

Johnathan Kana (Texas, US)

In God We Trust

Read 2 Corinthians 9:6–11

A generous person will prosper; whoever refreshes others will be refreshed.

Proverbs 11:25 (NIV)

The world economy is unstable. Too many of the world's people are in great need. But how can I be expected to help with so much uncertainty about the future? My family might have needs of our own; we don't know what's ahead. Fear-filled words fly at me from every direction. They nearly drown the one voice that speaks something radically different: 'Do not fear.'

As I listen to those words coming from the voice of God, I turn up the volume by opening my Bible. The words of scripture tell us we should not be hardhearted or tight-fisted with the poor (Deuteronomy 15:7); the one who gives to the poor will lack nothing (Proverbs 28:27); and Jesus says that as we give, it will be given back, overflowing (Luke 6:38).

In 1 Kings, Elijah asks a widow for a bit of bread. She has only a handful of flour and a little oil, but she gives it to the prophet. From then until Elijah leaves, her jars of oil and flour never run out.

Whom will I believe? Instead of the TV or newspaper, I choose to believe God who tells me I need not fear. I will give because I believe in God's promises.

Prayer: *Dear Lord, we want to be generous in giving even if things around us seem uncertain. Help us believe your voice of truth and not to be afraid. Amen*

Thought for the day: God's truth will drown out the sound of fear.

Link2Life: *Is there a food bank in your area to which you could give?*

Robin J. Steinweg (Wisconsin, US)

Our Perfect Prayer Partner

Read Romans 8:26–27

The Spirit helps us in our weakness; for we do not know how to pray as we ought.

Romans 8:26 (NRSV)

Several years ago, I had a faithful prayer partner. We met once a week and spent at least an hour in prayer. As word circulated about our meeting, other people gave us their lists of prayer requests. It was an exciting time.

My friend moved away, and I've had trouble finding someone who will make a commitment to a weekly prayer time. In our hustle-and-bustle world, finding a few moments of quiet is difficult.

However, even if we were alone on a desert island, we would have a prayer partner, one who knows how to reshape our prayers and to present them to God perfectly—the Holy Spirit. We may ask for things that might not be best for the person for whom we are praying. We cannot know how God is working in the life of any individual. But the Spirit knows.

Scripture teaches us that joining with other believers to pray is good; but when we cannot, we find comfort in knowing that the Spirit is always praying with us.

Prayer: *Dear God, thank you for the Holy Spirit's help in prayer. Amen*

Thought for the day: We never pray alone. The Spirit prays with us.

Mary A. Baird (Texas, US)

Never Lacking

Read Mark 6:30–44

To him who is able to do immeasurably more than all we ask or imagine, according to his power that is at work within us.
Ephesians 3:20 (NIV)

Twenty years ago, I went on my first short-term mission trip. I was a very young Christian then. Each of us on the team was asked to share a message at the end of the day to encourage one another. When it was my turn, I felt ill-equipped and lacking. I asked the Holy Spirit to guide me to a passage I could share. God led me to the simple passage where Jesus fed the multitudes. All he needed was five loaves and two fish and that was enough to satisfy the crowd of 5000.

That miracle spoke to me directly. We have nothing much to offer. We come as we are, sometimes lost, sometimes discouraged, and sometimes having little faith. But as long as we are willing to give all that we have, God will do the rest. As long as we are willing to surrender them completely, he will multiply what faith and talents we have to equip us with more than we need to bless those around us. Twenty years later, I'm still holding on to that truth. What a mighty and wonderful God we serve!

Prayer: *Dear Abba Father, increase our faith and bless the works of our hands so that we can be your light and salt in this world. In Jesus' name we pray. Amen*

Thought for the day: God's grace is sufficient for us (see 2 Corinthians 12:9).

Julie Sim (Singapore)

Remembering God

Read Deuteronomy 11:18–21

Write them on the doorframes of your houses and on your gates, so that your days and the days of your children may be many in the land the Lord swore to give your ancestors.

Deuteronomy 11:20–21 (NIV)

One night I began to scold my two daughters for taking too long to get to bed. It was getting late, and they had been told to hurry. Then I remembered that every evening they stop at their bedroom door to read the memory verse that one daughter pins up there. I stopped my scolding, knowing that following this simple reminder to memorise God's word was worth the delay.

Throughout the Bible we are given instructions about how to remember God. As a reminder of his awesome power and deliverance, God instructed Joshua to build a memorial (Joshua 4:1–22). Earlier God also instructed the Israelites with the words of today's verse.

Each of us can find a method for remembering God and put it into practice. My wife, Nancy, places little notes of scripture all over our house as reminders. What is crucial is not our memory method but that we remember who God is and how much we need him.

Prayer: *Dear Father in heaven, be with us each day, gently reminding us of who you are. Amen*

Thought for the day: What helps me remember God's presence in my life?

Link2Life: *Write out Bible verses and pin them up in your house.*

Jason A. Ponzio (Georgia, US)

Too Busy

Read Psalm 81:6–13

Recalling your tears, I long to see you, so that I may be filled with joy.
2 Timothy 1:4 (NIV)

My ageing mother lives alone and enjoys company from family and friends. Her world has shrunk considerably since my father died, and she seldom ventures out of the house except to go to the supermarket and the nearby pharmacy. Now and then she comments that her children don't call often enough. But when she said, 'I get homesick for my children', a sudden sadness melted my heart and her words prompted me to deeper reflection. Does God feel homesick for us?

The Israelites, God's chosen people, drifted away time after time; yet God never neglected them. Instead, he provided for them and corrected them. He was patient and fair. Why? Because the bonds between God and the people he loved brought him tremendous joy.

I suddenly longed to see Mum, to tell her that I loved her, to talk, to laugh and to enjoy her company.

Prayer: *Dear Father, please forgive our self-centred busyness. Help us to whittle away the unimportant events that consume our time. Help our actions to reflect what's in our hearts as we pray, 'Our Father which art in heaven, Hallowed be thy name. Thy kingdom come. Thy will be done, as in heaven, so in earth. Give us day by day our daily bread. And forgive us our sins; for we also forgive every one that is indebted to us. And lead us not into temptation; but deliver us from evil.'* Amen*

Thought for the day: Are you longing for a loved one? So is God.

Trudy K. Snyder (Pennsylvania, US)

Lighting a Candle

Read John 1:1–9

The light shines in the darkness, and the darkness did not overcome it.
John 1:9 (NRSV)

Some years ago my husband had a heart bypass operation. Coming home one day, I spoke with a neighbour who had recently moved near to us, and when I told her about my husband, she said gently, 'I will light a candle for him.' I thought that it was a very kind thing to do, and I was very moved by her words and simple gesture.

As the years passed my new neighbour became a dear friend. Later, when she moved into sheltered housing, and then when she was unable to get to church, she continued to light a candle, in her own home, for any she knew who were sick.

To me, this act is really a prayer, symbolic of light amid the darkness, and incorporating the thought that in our lives we should shine for Jesus. I've adopted the practice myself.

Prayer: *Dear Father God, help us every day to bring light into the lives of those around us, especially those who are ill, anxious or sad. Amen*

Thought for the day: Jesus wants us to shine in the world for him, creating light in the darkness.

Margaret Cook (West Lothian, Scotland)

Coincidence?

Read Hebrews 13:1–3
Do not quench the Spirit.
1 Thessalonians 5:19 (NIV)

Early one morning after a big storm, I looked up from my desk to see an agitated young man standing in the doorway of my office. When I invited him in, he sat down and poured out his troubles. He said he needed food and shelter, which I was able to help him with. Then he said that what he really needed was a new pair of sneakers since his had been ruined by walking in the heavy rain of the storm. I suggested a nearby charity shop, and he replied that he had been there and that they would not be open for four days.

Then the Holy Spirit nudged me to ask him what size sneaker he needed. He said that he wore size 12. That happened to be my size, so I said, 'Come with me.' We walked to the boot of my car where I retrieved the spare pair of size-12 sneakers that I always keep there. I handed them to him; he thanked me, and continued on his way.

I returned to my office, grateful that God had used me to help someone and awed at his wonderful timing. It reminded me that life's coincidences are often God's way of leading us to acts of service.

Prayer: *Ever-present God, we thank you for your guiding Spirit who helps us to look beyond ourselves to see the needs of others. Teach us to listen for your leading and give us the strength to follow. Amen*

Thought for the day: Our interruptions may be God's opportunities.

Richard Ryley (New York, US)

The Busy Bee

Read James 1:2–4
The testing of your faith produces endurance.
James 1:3 (NRSV)

While weeding in my garden, I watched an industrious bee buzzing from flower to flower. During this process, the pollen weighed the bee down as it gathered more and more of the gold dust on its body. I suddenly realised that in our lives we can carry around so many responsibilities that we can become weighed down too.

But there is a positive side to this story. The bee cross-pollinates as it flies from flower to flower, and it uses the nectar to make honey. Rather than allowing our concerns to weigh us down and create a negative state of mind, we can patiently change our focus and look at our struggles as opportunities from God. We have the opportunity to draw on our faith to find peace in the gospel of Christ—and then to carry that Good News from one life experience to another, even sharing the love, peace and joy of the Lord with everyone we meet. In this way we become a blessing wherever we go, just like the busy bee.

Prayer: *Lord Jesus, even when we are weighed down with responsibilities and worries, help us to spread your love and good news. Amen*

Thought for the day: Even when we are weighed down, we can be a blessing to others.

Kathleen A. Bradley (Florida, US)

Just a Wobble?

Read Psalm 1:1–6

[The believers] devoted themselves to the apostles' teaching and to fellowship, to the breaking of bread and to prayer.
Acts 2:42 (NIV)

As my husband, Jerry, and I went out for an early-morning bike ride, I noticed a broken spoke in my front wheel. I stopped and snapped it off the rim.

'Don't you think we should get that fixed?' Jerry asked.

'One missing spoke won't make a difference,' I declared.

At first, it didn't. For some time, the barely-noticeable wobble in the wheel had no effect on how the bicycle performed. After a few days, though, the wobble grew much worse. My husband was right in his concern; eventually I had to stop riding the bike because doing so posed a risk to my safety.

So it is with our spiritual life. At first, neglecting one of the spokes of spiritual disciplines in our lives—Bible study or prayer or worship or fellowship with other Christians—seems hardly to affect us. But over time, our lives may develop a decided wobble. And if we continue the neglect, our failure to pursue the things of God will have a profound impact on our relationship with God and others. The early church knew the value of spiritual disciplines. Scripture tells us they 'devoted themselves' to the pursuit of holy living. May we attend to the spokes in our spiritual lives and commit ourselves to keeping each of them strong.

Prayer: *O Lord, help us to be faithful in our daily walk with you. Amen*

Thought for the day: How will I pursue holy living today?

Beverly Varnado (Georgia, US)

Punctuation!

Read Psalm 23

He makes me lie down in green pastures.
Psalm 23:2 (NIV)

As writers, we are advised to make good use of punctuation and to avoid long sentences that ramble on and on. Both public speakers and preachers use the pause very successfully. But in our daily lives we tend to go on and on without a break, full of activity and busyness. 'Pausing' is not something we want to do.

My activities, instead of decreasing with the passing years, had been increasing. I didn't complain for, as a widow, it helped me to be busy, especially as I felt it was all for the Lord. But gently the Lord reminded me that in our lives there is also a need for 'punctuation'. As 'he gives his beloved sleep' (Psalm 127:2, KJV) so sometimes he 'makes us lie down' (Psalm 23:2, NIV).

We are exhorted in the Bible to give thanks in every circumstance and, though it is hard, I know I must learn to trust God and therefore give thanks to him for the pauses in life as well as the busy times. Perhaps the quiet time only represents a semi-colon and I will soon be out and about again. But a full stop may mean the end of a paragraph or even a chapter.

It is good to know that it is Jesus who is the author and finisher of our faith. He is writing a wonderful story—yes, even through our lives—and it will bring him glory throughout endless ages. So let us trust him with the punctuation of our lives too.

Prayer: *Lord, help us to trust you when things do not work out the way we had hoped, and to know that even in our weakness our strength is in you. Amen*

Thought for the day: Jesus is the author and finisher of our faith.

Pauline Lewis (South Wales, United Kingdom)

Bold Faith

Read Luke 10:1–12

[The mob] dragged Jason and some believers before the city authorities, shouting, 'These people who have been turning the world upside down have come here also.'
Acts 17:6 (NRSV)

Some of my neighbours park their cars on the side of the road at the crest of a hill. Those who want to drive past them have to swing out with no idea who or what might be coming toward them. It makes driving in our neighbourhood quite an adventure.

This example of bad parking is actually a pretty good representation of our life in God. Faith is not for the faint-hearted. We are asked to start a journey, without necessarily knowing where we are going or what might be coming toward us. We are not given a map; rather, we are asked to trust that we are going somewhere good. The 'danger' of this journey is unlikely to result in smashed bumpers or broken bones, but it may well breach our comfortable lives.

We can't imagine all the possibilities that time and life may bring to us, but faith can be exhilarating! What God has in store for us is probably more breathtaking than anything we could come up with on our own. I've always believed that the serious Christian life is for the adventurous. The journey, if we're brave enough to take it, is never dull.

Prayer: *Reassuring God, give us the courage to go where you lead even though we don't know what the journey will bring. Amen*

Thought for the day: Faith calls for a sense of adventure!

Nancy Johnson (Georgia, US)

Legacy of Faith

Read Psalm 71:1–9

Recite [these words that I am commanding you today] to your children and talk about them when you are at home and when you are away, when you lie down and when you rise.

Deuteronomy 6:7 (NRSV)

Last year I celebrated the 'threescore years and ten' spoken of in Psalm 90:10 (KJV). When I look in the mirror, I see with some regret my sagging muscles, wrinkled skin and my grey balding head. I am reminded of the potions, pills and guaranteed cures for these conditions that assail me from the screen of my TV and from the pages of newspapers and magazines. Temptation is there, but instead of trying to renovate the old, I observe with excitement and joy the vibrant, young extension of my life in my children and grandchildren.

I do not mourn my gradually fading memory. Instead, I use my remaining God-given resources and spiritual gifts joyfully, to ensure that through my example of prayer and love my descendants and others may see Christ in me. I want them to follow in the path of joy and peace that I have known in my Christian life. In the fullness of time they will follow me to be with God for ever.

Prayer: *Dear God, thank you for your blessings of love and joy. Help us to pass these on to the generations who follow us. Amen*

Thought for the day: No matter what age we achieve, we are always God's children.

Keith Honeyman (Cape Town, South Africa)

PRAYER FOCUS: THOSE WHO ARE AGEING ALONE

God is Able

Read Exodus 3:1–10

The angel of the Lord appeared to [Moses] in flames of fire from within a bush.

Exodus 3:2 (NIV)

Frustrated by feelings of uncertainty, I cried out to God: 'What do you want me to do? I'm trying to be useful, but I'm not sure I'm using my time and talents in the best way!' Though I volunteer at church and in my community, I thought perhaps I was missing something. How do I know if I'm on the right track? How can I be sure I won't miss God's call?

In the midst of my prayer, an image of a burning bush came into my mind. I remembered how God came to Moses while Moses was tending sheep in the wilderness. Though Moses was far away from his homeland, God found him, used a burning bush to get his attention, and then told him exactly what to do. God met Moses exactly where he was and spoke in words that he could understand.

I felt relief as I realised that God knows where I am too. If there is something else I should be doing, he is powerful enough to let me know. I don't need to fear I'll miss it, but can rest in the truth that God knows how to reach me—perhaps through a phone call from a friend, an announcement, a news story or another burning bush! Whatever method God chooses, I can trust that he is able to communicate clearly to me the next step on my journey.

Prayer: *Dear Father, thank you for knowing where we are and for calling us to help you as you work in this world. Amen*

Thought for the day: God knows where I am and what I can do.

Lynn Karidis (Michigan, US)

Loving Your Neighbour

Read Mark 12:28–31

The entire law is fulfilled in keeping this one command: 'Love your neighbour as yourself.'
Galatians 5:14 (NIV)

My wife, Stephanie, and I recently moved to a new area of the country where we knew almost no one. This was difficult for us because we had always lived surrounded by friends and family. One hot summer evening soon after we moved, we went for a walk through our neighbourhood and were nearly home. Sweaty and dirty, we saw a couple carrying groceries from their car. We stopped and talked for a few minutes, and then they invited us in for dinner. At first we hesitated and asked if we could go home to clean up and change clothes before returning for dinner. They insisted that we come in just as we were. We shared a lovely time of fellowship while eating a delicious meal.

Didn't these new friends do what we as Christians are commanded to do—love our neighbours simply as they are? They didn't judge us; they simply saw two human beings to whom they could show God's love. God calls us to show this same type of love to the world around us. Each of us can find endless opportunities to express his love. All we have to do is have the faith and courage to respond according to his call to love our neighbours as ourselves.

Prayer: *Dear God, help each of us to spread your love to those around us, treating them with the love and respect that you have graciously given to us. Amen*

Thought for the day: People notice when we love as Christ loves.

Link2Life: *Invite someone new to your church or area over for a meal.*

Zach Fitzpatrick (Kentucky, US)

PRAYER FOCUS: NEW PEOPLE IN MY COMMUNITY

Autumn Leaves

Read Philippians 4:4–9
You, O Lord, have made me glad by your work; at the works of your hands I sing for joy.
Psalm 92:4 (NRSV)

In our region of the world the autumn leaves are glorious. The green leaves turn to shades of yellow, red and orange. Landscapes turn to canvasses that only God could paint. The colours are so brilliant, they are breathtaking. My husband and I enjoy seeing the glorious colours in nature. Even quick trips to the shops are more pleasant because of the beauty of autumn. Some people, however, dread the season because of the work of raking up the leaves, and they overlook its spectacular beauty.

The mood of a day is often set by our focus. If we focus on our problems, our mood is likely to be glum. If we focus on the Lord's blessings, then in spite of our problems, we can see each day as a day that the Lord has made and we can rejoice and be glad (Psalm 118:24). If we sing for joy at the beauty of autumn leaves, raking them up will be all the more enjoyable. As I rake leaves, I thank God for making them beautiful so that the task is less of a burden. If we sing for joy in all God's works, our songs will lighten our load and make our trials easier to bear.

Prayer: *Dear God, thank you for the changing seasons and for the work of your hands that gives us joy. Amen*

Thought for the day: Focusing on God's joy makes our trials easier to bear.

Mary K. Gulledge (Ohio, US)

The Present Moment

Read Esther 4:1–17

Mordecai [told] Esther, 'Who knows? Perhaps you have come to royal dignity for just such a time as this.'
Esther 4:14 (NRSV)

Last summer I was in Africa, and I gained a completely new understanding of time. One day we were expected at events in two different churches. When we got to the first church I asked my host, 'When will we need to leave here in order to get to our next appointment on time?' He answered, 'We will leave here when we are ready! We need to give our full attention to these people here now, and we cannot do that if we are already thinking about where we are going next.'

After pondering the host's answer, I realised just how difficult it is to live in the present. I love to reflect on the past or dream about the future, but the present can pass me by all too easily. Today's Bible reading from the Book of Esther speaks about living in the present moment. Esther understood that by leaving the past behind and not being afraid of the future, she was able to give herself completely to the present moment and to those people who needed her at that particular time.

Prayer: *Dear Lord, give us this day our daily bread. Amen*

Thought for the day: God's gift of today is irreplaceable.

Nicola Vidamour (London, England)

What We Know is True

Read 2 Timothy 3:10–17

All scripture is inspired by God and is useful for teaching, for reproof, for correction, and for training in righteousness.

2 Timothy 3:16 (NRSV)

Recently, I flew to a small town in Alaska—a beautiful land of snow, ice, moose and bear. I had hoped it would be a clear day so I could see a glacier or two or maybe a herd of moose or caribou. Instead, it was snowing, and the dark grey day offered little visibility.

The plane was small, with no door between us and the pilots. As I looked up where the pilots sat, I realised that for the entire flight they could not see anything through their windscreen. Instead, they relied on their instruments to guide our flight.

I could not help but think about how we act and react when we are going through the storms and turmoil of life and cannot see the future. When we cannot see how we are going to make it, we can trust what we know to be true: God is with us. He hears our prayers, sees our tears and wants to guide us. Just as those pilots could not see what was ahead of them, we can't see the future, but we can trust the guidance we find in God's word.

Prayer: *Thank you, God, for the truth you reveal to us in your word. Thank you for Jesus, who brought your truth to life. Amen*

Thought for the day: We can face the future because God is there.

Andy Baker (Tennessee, US)

Around the World

Read Psalm 67:1–7

As you, Father, are in me and I am in you, may they also be in us, so that the world may believe that you have sent me.
John 17:21 (NRSV)

When I open my computer each morning I'm excited to read the meditation from *The Upper Room*. Not only do I get a message that guides or uplifts me during the day; I also have fellowship with Christians all over the world. I have a chance to pray for the circumstances of the authors—for their bereavement, struggles of faith or rejoicing.

I pray next for the country where the day's writer lives. Recently I have prayed for Japan, Germany, Spain, Australia, Canada and my own country, England. The various US states have been featured in my prayers as well. On my wall hangs a large map of the world to help me locate the countries I'm not very familiar with.

Each morning I get a thrill as I realise that people all over the world are reading these same scripture passages and the meditations and praying about the same concerns. Though we read and pray at different times, our problems, searching and rejoicing are similar, and we all can receive answers and help as we read. And because we read and pray at different times, as we do, a wave of prayer moves around the globe.

Whatever our circumstances and wherever we are, God is the same—faithful to hear us.

Prayer: *All praise to you, faithful God, that you listen to us and have compassion on us. Amen*

Thought for the day: When I read here each day and pray, I become part of a circle of the faithful that reaches around the world.

Carol Purves (Cumbria, England)

Adapting with Grace

Read Genesis 12:1–9

God is our refuge and strength… Therefore we will not fear, though the earth should change, though the mountains shake.
Psalm 46:1–2 (NRSV)

We were climbing in the mountains in the state of Washington and our plan was simple: on Monday we would climb Mount St Helens for its spectacular views. On Tuesday, we'd climb Mount Rainier to just below the snow level. But at St Helens, the summit and our view were shrouded by clouds. On Mount Rainier, the path we had planned to take was covered with twelve feet of snow. We had to adapt.

In many areas of life we have to adapt, sometimes to unwelcome realities. Moving beyond asking 'Why?' to discerning 'What now?' requires letting God lead us into a new way of life. He never leaves us in a place where grace cannot sustain us. We live in a world that won't always go the way we expect it to go; sometimes adapting ourselves is the best, most faithful response we can make.

If we trust in God's enduring love in Jesus Christ as our faithful companion, teacher and guide, and rely on the power of the Holy Spirit, we will have what we need to face any change.

Prayer: *O Christ, faithful guide, teach us to look for you and trust your guidance when life forces us onto unexpected paths as we pray, 'Father, hallowed be your name, your kingdom come. Give us each day our daily bread. Forgive us our sins, for we also forgive everyone who sins against us. And lead us not into temptation.'* Amen*

Thought for the day: Adapting to change can be a faithful response.

F. Richard Garland (Rhode Island, US)

PRAYER FOCUS: THOSE FACING UNWANTED CHANGE
* Luke 11:2–4 (NIV)

Standing the Test of Time

Read Ecclesiastes 2:9–11

Even when I am old and grey, do not forsake me, O God, till I declare your power to the next generation, your might to all who are to come.
Psalm 71:18 (NIV)

My husband and I have begun researching our family history. During this process we have visited many cemeteries to take pictures of family gravestones. Some are simple, small headstones. Others are grand monuments. Many quote a scripture verse, or say how much the person was loved and will be missed.

The passing of time, however, has been an enemy to these well-intentioned memorials. Many are fading, falling down, broken and cracked. Some plots are covered over with grass, and not all monuments are readable.

If King David and King Solomon had grand burial sites, time and generations have hidden the locations. But their failures and victories, their works of faith that live on in the psalms and writings in the Bible, remind us of our need for God.

Memorials of stone, marble and brass may not last. But our life of faith and the example we set will be passed down from generation to generation—a permanent monument that will stand the test of time.

Prayer: *Dear Father, help us to live in a way that those who come after us will find in our lives true examples of faith in you. Amen*

Thought for the day: What spiritual legacy will I leave to others?

Shelby H. Grant (North Carolina, US)

New Life

Read John 15:1–11

Jesus said, 'Abide in me as I abide in you.'
John 15:4 (NRSV)

A few days ago I was surprised to find a butterfly lying on our small patio. It did not move, and I thought it was dead. I carefully picked it up to show my young daughters, and together we admired the delicate wings and antennae. I placed the butterfly on a table, out of my daughters' reach. After a while, I noticed that the butterfly was in a different position. My husband suggested that I place it in the sunlight because the temperatures of the previous few days might have left it very cold. I did so, and after a few minutes the butterfly was fluttering its wings. It was alive!

Something similar can happen to us when we fall away from our communion with God and our brothers and sisters in Christ. We fail to pray regularly, read God's word, or give him praise and thanks. Our spirit begins to 'chill', and we no longer reflect the life of Christ.

However, when we return to God, the Light and the Truth, in his presence and with his people, our spiritual strength will return. We will then be ready to praise and serve God and to reflect his wondrous love.

Prayer: *God of all creation, help us remain close to you and to leave behind all that distracts us from you and the community of faith. Amen*

Thought for the day: No matter how chilled we become, God's love never wanes.

Lucy de Tamez (Virginia, US)

Beloved of God

Read Luke 3:21–22

A voice from heaven said to Jesus, 'You are my Son, whom I love; with you I am well pleased.'
Luke 3:22 (NIV)

Quietly, over a number of months, I fell into the bad habit of allowing myself to be dragged down into a pit of worry and despair. I began to worry even when I had nothing to worry about. This habit led to pessimism that was not helpful to me, my family or others around me.

By grace, I found Luke 3:21–22, in which John baptises people. God's Holy Spirit descends on Jesus in the form of a dove, and a voice speaks directly to Jesus saying, 'You are my Son, whom I love; with you I am well pleased' (Luke 3:22). In this profound moment, Jesus' identity was confirmed.

These days, when worry and doubt begin to assail me, I have a new way of dealing with them. Over and over again I repeat these words: 'You are my beloved. With you I am well pleased.' In a world of distraction and noise, I find it helpful to remember that God loves me.

When times get tough and the world seems to weigh us down, we can remind each other that we are God's beloved children. And God is pleased with us.

Prayer: *Thank you, God, for Jesus Christ, through whom we have all been called your beloved. Amen*

Thought for the day: Today I will remember that I am God's beloved.

Roland P. Rink (Gauteng, South Africa)

ABC Prayers

Read Philippians 1:3–11

Paul wrote, 'I thank God, whom I serve, as my ancestors did, with a clear conscience, as night and day I constantly remember you in my prayers.'
2 Timothy 1:3 (NIV)

For some reason I have been waking up in the middle of the night, staring at the ceiling and wondering why I am awake. I'm tired. I have to get up early. What am I to do?

A few nights ago, I remembered a friend's suggestion about ABC prayers. I began with the letter A and thought of people whose name begins with A. Then I prayed specifically for their needs and asked God to touch their lives. Then I moved on to B. I remember reaching the letter M, but the rest is a blur. I was sleeping peacefully again.

This exercise reminds me of the joy and peace we find in praying for others. In our small Bible study group, we collect weekly prayer requests. We have been amazed to see the power of our prayers at work. Talking with God and submitting our sincere requests for his help and guidance for our friends and family leads to amazing results or even, as in my case, a calming and peaceful repose.

Prayer: *Dear God, thank you for hearing our prayers at all times of the day or night. Amen*

Thought for the day: We receive unexpected blessings when we meet God in prayer.

Link2Life: *Begin your own 'alphabet of prayer'.*

Sherah B. Carr (Georgia, US)

Unappreciative?

Read John 21:15–17

Jesus said to [Peter], 'Feed my lambs.'

John 21:15 (NRSV)

When I began serving at a homeless shelter, I assumed the guests would be appreciative. But several complained about the menu, and others snatched their plates in silence. Most met my smile with sideways glances that spoke of wariness and distrust. I thought angrily, 'How dare they treat me this way? They don't even know me.'

Then I heard God speaking through my frustration: 'Jill, do you know them?' The next week I began actually to sit and eat with the guests. I asked, 'How are you?' and took the time to listen—not only to what was said but also to what was not said. I heard the sadness in the tone of voice, observed the forced smile and was touched by the eyes filled with tears. I learned names and heard stories. Those I once saw only as grouchy and ungrateful became sisters and brothers each with their own unique pains of the past, fears of the present and hopes for the future.

In our reading for today, Jesus gave Simon some very specific directions about showing his love for Christ by serving others: 'Feed my lambs... Tend my sheep.' Even those who at first seem unappreciative, we are also called to feed and to tend.

Prayer: *Dear God, help us discover how we might tend to the physical and spiritual needs of the people around us. Amen*

Thought for the day: Serving in Christ's name requires building relationships.

Jill Allen Maisch (Maryland, US)

Prayer Workshop

Writing as Prayer: Psalms

As a chaplain at a hospital, I sit with people from all walks of life through the extreme and the mundane, the joyous and the sorrowful. When asked to teach a spiritual practice to our patients, I searched for a biblically-based practice that could speak to a wide variety of people. It was one of my older patients who unknowingly helped me. Telling me how he loved the Psalms, he explained: 'I tried to take my brother's wife. I've also been betrayed. All the time I was behaving badly and scared, I still loved God. All the things I've shouted out to God, King David shouted out too. It's different, but it's the same, as if I'm reading my own prayers.'

From this encounter came the inspiration to write psalms as a way to pray. I have begun writing psalms as prayers in my own journal. In individual pastoral counselling, I often encourage patients to write a psalm about whatever matter we have discussed. When we conclude, I read the psalm aloud as a spoken prayer, a way to bless our shared spiritual endeavour and lift our work to God.

The topics of the Psalms reflect our timeless spiritual need for meaning and purpose. We need to know that God is near in good times and bad, in praise and in lamentation, when we're getting things right or making a mess of them. The Psalms encourage us to come before God exactly as we are, today.

When I took up the practice myself, I began to see that writing psalms from my life gave me a new perspective. I sometimes get caught up in negative thinking, ruminating over hurts or mistakes. This is almost impossible to do when writing a psalm. Even when the psalmist is writing about a deeply negative subject matter, such as betrayal in Psalm 55 or deep personal sin repented as in Psalm 51, the psalmist does not simply state the grim facts but also thinks of a future in which God has restored and renewed life with grace and abundant love. Being able to write one's darkest doubts or worst fears and then imagining God providing a way out of them is one of the gifts that writing psalms can offer.

Writing psalms of trust and confidence is a powerful way to deepen our faith. We can think of new ways to put our faith in God despite boredom, confusion or tragedy. Notice in Psalm 23 that three lines are devoted to images of God's grace and protection before the single line stating, 'I walk through the valley of the shadow of death...'. This single image of difficulty is potent. Yet the images of trust, deliverance, hope and security are just as potent. In six different images, we see the ways in which the Lord acts as the Divine Shepherd, sheltering us. The psalmist concludes with the faith that no matter where this life leads, God's goodness and mercy follow him; God is his home. Several meditations in this issue offer reflections on finding hope and faith even in difficult situations. You may want to re-read the meditations for 6, 8, 15, 16, 20 and 22 September, 19, 20 and 26 October, 2 and 8 November and 14, 17 and 30 December before writing your own psalm using the instructions below.

Perhaps you have already seen ways in which you might use the psalms to spark your own 'shouting out' to God. If not, I hope you find some of these writing prompts fruitful. Use the Psalms as inspiration to write your own psalms, your own prayers. Once you get the idea of what your heart longs to give to God in word, go with it. Remember, each psalm reminds us that we can come before God as we are because he is for us, bearing with us and loving us.

Questions for reflection

1. Reflect on a time of difficulty and find an image of what it looked like (or would look like) for you to come through that time. Write a psalm in which you state three ways you lived through this difficulty for every one way you describe the difficulty: For example:

O Lord, the wind swept away all that we had saved and there was nothing,
Out of an empty kitchen you showed me there was food for us.
You put back together our broken hearts.
Where our tears fell, you planted joys to grow as numerous as the stars.

2. Read Psalm 100. Think about what it means for God's love to be what defines you: your life's meaning and purpose is to be God's beloved. Nothing else exceeds this. Write a psalm about entering God's presence and fully experiencing your own soul as the beloved of God. For the psalmist this looked like a jubilant court entrance. What does it look like to you? A day in the garden? A table set with food for all? The candlelit silence of a grand cathedral?

3. Read Psalm 65. Reflect on the smallness of human life amidst the grand scale of the earth, stars and cosmos. Write a psalm affirming your life's meaning and purpose as a created child of God inhabiting this great, wide world.

4. Read Psalm 28 and then put it away. Reflect on a need you experience. Begin your psalm with three descriptions of the Lord delivering you from this need. Describe your need only once, as vividly as possible. Conclude your psalm with expressions of thanksgiving that your need has been met.

Jane M. Herring, a former teacher, received an M.Div. from Vanderbilt University Divinity School in Nashville, Tennessee. Her companions on life's journey are her husband and daughter, two dogs, one cat and family far and wide. Jane had a deep interest in spiritual formation before she even knew what the words meant. She is currently a hospital chaplain in clinical pastoral care.

All Saints' Day

Read Ephesians 1:15–23

Ever since I heard about your faith in the Lord Jesus and your love for all the saints, I have not stopped giving thanks for you.

Ephesians 1:15–16 (NIV)

All Saints' Sunday in our church has always been important to me. During this special service we remember all those of our church family who have died during the past year. We rejoice in the fact that they have attained the promise of eternal life with God. As I reflect back on the lives of these people and the saints honoured in previous years, I remember their involvement in the life of the church. Many of them were quite active—teaching, working in missions, serving in various capacities and remaining faithful in their worship and Bible study. They have 'in everything set… an example by doing what is good' (Titus 2:7). Each of these people, in his or her way, has had a great impact on me and my faith walk.

All Saints' Day causes me to stop and think about my own life. How will the generation that follows me be influenced by my service and my witness? Am I making a positive contribution to the lives of this community of believers? This special day gives me a renewed desire to follow Christ more fully as did the saints who went before me.

Prayer: *Dearest heavenly Father, help us to remember that others may be looking to us as models of faith. Guide us to be ever mindful of our actions that we may be examples of what is good. Amen*

Thought for the day: Walking in the footsteps of the saints leads to true worship of God.

Jeanne C. Gore (North Carolina, US)

Even There

Read Psalm 139:1–18
In [the Lord's] hand is the life of every living thing and the breath of every human being.
Job 12:10 (NRSV)

My daughter's poor health was becoming a growing concern, and the doctors seemed unable to find a solution. Someone suggested that moving to a more favourable climate might be beneficial. Although I fully supported every hope for improvement, as a parent I mourned her leaving. Giving up my active role as her carer and giving her the freedom to put down roots 3000 miles away were difficult lessons in how to trust and let go.

However, God is patient, kind and attentive to the cries of my heart. Reading the Bible and prayerful meditation assure me that we can never travel farther than God's healing presence. His abiding love will always be with us. No matter where we call home, even there God will hold us in the palm of his hand.

Prayer: *Thank you, Lord, for hearing the cries of our hearts and giving us your healing grace and peace. We pray as Jesus taught us, saying, 'Our Father in heaven, hallowed be your name, your kingdom come, your will be done, on earth as it is in heaven. Give us today our daily bread. And forgive us our debts, as we also have forgiven our debtors. And lead us not into temptation, but deliver us from the evil one.'* Amen*

Thought for the day: God's abiding love helps us learn to trust.

Ellen Adams (Virginia, US)

PRAYER FOCUS: SOMEONE SUFFERING WITH A CHRONIC ILLNESS
* Matthew 6:9–13 (NIV)

All-weather Commitment

Read Luke 14:26–33

Jesus said to them… 'If any want to become my followers, let them deny themselves and take up their cross daily and follow me.'
Luke 9:23 (NRSV)

One hot, sunny day I was out in the garden, mowing our lawn. Eventually I noticed Ben, our Labrador, following me. He easily could have gone into the garage—where it wasn't as hot—and lapped up a drink of water to cool down, but our loyal dog continued to follow me in the heat, panting profusely.

When I thought about Ben's commitment to following me, the question came to mind: am I that committed to following Christ? When things in my life aren't going well or when the Lord doesn't answer one of my prayers the way I would like, am I still committed to following him? Or am I loyal to Christ only when everything in life is going my way? Our dog's commitment to following me, in spite of tough circumstances, challenged me to be more devoted in my commitment to follow Christ.

Prayer: *Dear God, give us your grace and strength to be committed to you even when life is full of trials. Amen*

Thought for the day: Is my commitment to Christ conditional?

Tyler Myers (Ohio, US)

Slippers or Shoes?

Read Psalm 63:1–8

Very early in the morning, while it was still dark, Jesus got up, left the house and went off to a solitary place, where he prayed.
Mark 1:35 (NIV)

A wail came from the back seat of the car as we left home for a day out. 'I've got my slippers on!' my niece lamented. Somehow in the excitement of the anticipated day, my niece had simply scampered into the car forgetting to change into her shoes, or indeed to prepare in any way.

We still tease my niece about that incident at times, but it is a good reminder to me of the need to be prepared and to be spiritually ready for the day ahead. Having only my slippers on would mean I was ill-equipped and inappropriately dressed. Likewise, if I'm to be ready to follow God's truths in this needy world, I need to spend time in prayer and in focusing on God's word at the start of the day. How easy it is to rush into a new day without stopping to be properly prepared! Jesus set the best example. May God give all of us the grace to recognise our need and to make the time to be spiritually well-dressed!

Prayer: *Dear Father, today we seek your forgiveness, your protection, your enabling power and strength for all this day will bring. Amen*

Thought for the day: Put on the full armour of God (see Ephesians 6:11).

Hilary Allen (Somerset, England)

Blessed Are the Humble

Read Matthew 5:1–12
Blessed are the poor in spirit, for theirs is the kingdom of heaven.
Matthew 5:3 (NRSV)

I had just completed several frustrating trips around the hospital car park looking for a space when I saw a man heading for his car. I positioned myself to move into his space, which I, of course, considered mine. Suddenly a young woman quickly and expertly manoeuvred her car around several parked cars and into the space I was waiting for. The woman hastily got out of her car, flashed me a smile and moved off rapidly toward the hospital. I don't know what she meant to communicate with her smile, but I gave it a very negative interpretation as I sat there feeling annoyed.

Later, in my quiet time with the Lord, I realised my reaction should have been much kinder. Perhaps the woman was in the midst of a life-threatening emergency, and her smile was an appeal for me to understand or to forgive her. Whatever the situation, I realised I needed to respond in a way that was pleasing to the Lord. Jesus, with infinite wisdom, gave us the guidelines and directions in the Beatitudes that would help us to live humbly and be more like him. And in 1 Peter 5:5 we read, 'All of you must clothe yourselves with humility in your dealings with one another, for "God opposes the proud, but gives grace to the humble".'

Prayer: *Dear Lord, help us to live humbly and to be your witnesses in all circumstances. Amen*

Thought for the day: Hasty assumptions can derail Christ-like actions.

Walter N. Maris (Missouri, US)

Dancing My Prayers

Read Psalm 149:1–4
David, wearing a linen ephod, danced before the Lord with all his might.
2 Samuel 6:14 (NIV)

As a Native American, I have the honour and privilege of carrying on the tradition of Native American dancing. Within each dance step runs a deep connection among my ancestors, those who live now and the generations to come. My spirit-filled dance gives honour and praise to God, while giving me a way to offer my prayers to my Creator.

The dress I wear is called a jingle-dance or prayer-dance dress. The cones on the dress represent prayers. As I dance, each cone hits another and the prayers sing out their requests to God. A servicewoman in our armed forces gave me this dress when she returned from her first tour of duty in Iraq. Her handwritten message said that the prayers on the dress were for the soldiers who served side by side with her and for the families of those who did not return home. She told me always to dance for peace and healing.

Each time I dance, whether it is for a Native American ministry Sunday service, pow-wow or a gathering to share our Native ways, my tear-filled eyes dance with pride, as I honour the prayers of those I do not know. My dress reminds me that any act done in love on behalf of another is a kind of prayer.

Prayer: *Creator God, we thank you for hearing our prayers, in whatever language we offer them. Amen*

Thought for the day: Any act of love can be a prayer.

Boe Harris-Nakakakena (Delaware, US)

Precious to God

Read Isaiah 43:1–7

You are precious in my sight, and honoured, and I love you.
Isaiah 43:4 (NRSV)

A few years ago, I moved to a new country for a new job. I felt excited at first, but later I became discouraged due to the challenges I was facing. Communication differences hindered my fitting into the new environment. I found meeting people's expectations difficult, and I started to feel that I was not good enough for the new company I was working for. I began to lose confidence and to question my self-worth. Fear and anxiety found their way into my heart.

In the midst of my despair, God's words in Isaiah 43:4 lifted me up and renewed my spirit. I remembered that I am precious to God and that he accepts me as I am, no matter what people think or say. The truth of God's enduring love helped me to regain my confidence in life. Since I know that I am precious in God's sight, I can rest assured that he will deliver me from any circumstances.

Nothing about our problems is too small for God. We can overcome our problems with the strength of the Lord, who lives in us.

Prayer: *Dear God, thank you for accepting us. Help us to accept others as you have accepted us. Amen*

Thought for the day: I am loved, honoured and precious in God's sight.

Edi Saputra (Singapore)

Delight in the Lord

Read Psalm 98:1–9
Take delight in the Lord and he will give you the desires of your heart.
Psalm 37:4 (NIV)

What does it mean to take delight in the Lord? I have struggled with this question over the years, wondering if I experienced delight in my relationship with the Lord. First, I thought about my children and the feelings of joy and pleasure as I watch them grow and mature. I thought of how I rejoice in a sunset or sunrise, how I thrill to be able to ride a horse, and how I take pleasure in a walk through the woods after a fresh rain. I ponder the feelings of exultation that overtake me when I reunite with a friend. I take delight in all these circumstances.

Next, I consider how my heart reacts in worship services at church. My response is often joy, excitement and pleasure. I am reminded of who God is when I sing in the fellowship of other believers. In my considerations, I realised that I experience pleasure in the Lord not only during worship, but also when I delight in my children, in God's creation and in my friends. Finally I rejoice in God, who is Lord of all. All of life is an occasion to delight in the Lord.

Prayer: *Dear God, make us aware of your presence in all our experiences. May we delight in you wherever we find you. Amen*

Thought for the day: Each day presents opportunities to delight in God.

Link2Life: *Make a list of the things that bring you joy in your faith, and thank God for them.*

Tara H. West (Ohio, US)

Three Little Words

Read 1 John 4:7–21

We love because [God] first loved us.
1 John 4:19 (NRSV)

Growing up, I never heard my parents say that they loved my brother, my sister or me. I'm sure they did love us. It's just that, for whatever reasons, saying those three little words, 'I love you', must have been hard for them. A few years ago, my wife and I flew to Florida where my mother was in a retirement home. She was quite ill. I wanted to see her and to tell her I loved her, maybe for the last time. I did, and I felt good about it. My mother was somewhat uncomfortable and only said, 'Goodbye', nothing more. I suppose saying 'I love you' was still too hard for her.

Every day, I make sure that my boys hear, from my heart and from my lips, how much I love them. They need to know. I need to tell them. These words are nice to hear—and to say.

God says 'I love you' throughout the Bible. His word is crystal clear in declaring his love for us, which is demonstrated in the gift of Jesus Christ. God is never ashamed to tell us how much we are loved.

Prayer: *Dear Lord, thank you for loving us in your only Son, Jesus Christ. Amen*

Thought for the day: Today I will speak words of love—as God does.

John Adam Fischer (Washington, US)

In Love with the World?

Read Mark 8:34–38

Jesus said, 'Everyone therefore who acknowledges me before others, I also will acknowledge before my Father in heaven; but whoever denies me before others, I will also deny before my Father in heaven.'
Matthew 10:32–33 (NRSV)

For most of my adult life I was a devoted atheist. I would tell anyone who would listen that God made no sense; it seemed easy to defend my views. Shortly after my conversion, however, I was presented with the opportunity to defend Christ to a colleague who was espousing the same views I had once held. I choked. Suddenly, I was more concerned about what my friend thought of me than what was important to Christ. In that moment I discovered that I was more in love with the world than with God.

Scripture teaches that those who are in love with the world do not have the Father's love in them (see 1 John 2:15). We Christians too often are concerned about what our peers will think if we share our faith in Christ. Christ Jesus, however, instructs us to share our faith boldly and promises to be with us always (see Matthew 28:18–20).

I regret those days when I hesitated to share my faith; I regret having ever turned my back on Christ. There are no magical words or formulas needed to tell others about our faith in Christ. All that's needed is honesty and a willingness to tell others what Christ has done in our lives. In the end, we will be rewarded for loving God more.

Prayer: *Ever-living God, give us confidence to be your witnesses in the world. Grant us the courage to love you more than we love the world. Amen*

Thought for the day: We can ask God for courage in difficult times.

Clark Goble (Ohio, US)

Set Prisoners Free

Read Psalm 103:7–18

Jesus said, 'Father, forgive them, for they do not know what they are doing.'

Luke 23:34 (NIV)

For years, I thought that to forgive you must forget. How can I forgive someone, I reasoned, if I don't forget what they've done to me? Yet for me, forgetting seemed impossible—for the scenario of their wrongdoing would keep playing in my head.

One day I realised that forgiving is a purposeful and deliberate act. We won't forget the misdeed, but we can choose to forgive the person anyway. That is forgiving the way our Father forgives us. God surely never forgets our sins, but chooses to wipe the slate clean each day as we ask for forgiveness.

Corrie Ten Boom, who helped to hide Jews in Holland during the Second World War, once said, 'Forgiveness is to set a prisoner free, and to realise that the prisoner was you.' God intentionally chooses to set us free—free to love in spite of what we have experienced. This is what it means to forgive like our Father and our Lord Jesus Christ.

Prayer: *Our Father, thank you for wiping the slate clean, intentionally forgiving us, starting us anew. May we follow your example of wiping the slate clean for others. Amen*

Thought for the day: God sets us free to forgive and to love.

Nancy Payton Brown (South Carolina, US)

A Light in the Darkness

Read Lamentations 3:19–26

Your word is a lamp to my feet and a light for my path.
Psalm 119:105 (NIV)

The word 'cancer' provokes dark emotions: fear, anxiety and a sense of doom, to name but a few. When I was diagnosed with breast cancer, these words from Lamentations and Psalm 119 became the lamp that shone God's light along my path.

There were times when I realised how powerful and comforting the prayers of strangers can be, particularly during periods of great physical, emotional and spiritual weakness. All strength and resolve seemed to dissolve into a haze of voices, medication sickness, emptiness and profound loneliness. I woke in pain many times in the early hours when others had gone to bed, feeling scared and alone. But then I would settle back into bed, feeling and knowing that I was being prayed for by my brothers and sisters across the world. It was as though I was being held by a thousand hands.

Sometimes we have to reach what feels like the end of ourselves before we can fully comprehend how high, how deep and wide is God's love for us. These words from Lamentations remind us of this: 'His compassions never fail. They are new every morning; great is your faithfulness' (Lamentations 3:22–23).

Prayer: *Dear Father, thank you for your love, joy, peace and comfort shown to us through your word. Help us to shine your light into the lives of those going through dark times. Amen*

Thought for the day: God's word comforts and guides us through all our daily challenges.

Gina Matthews (Hampshire, England)

Being First

Read Mark 10:35–45

Sitting down, Jesus called the Twelve and said, 'Anyone who wants to be first must be the very last, and the servant of all.'
Mark 9:35 (NIV)

'Be the first to own the newest computer on the market!' As I read the advertisement, I paused to reflect on how much emphasis is placed on being first. People stand in a queue for days to be the first to own the latest electronic device. Others spend long hours at work to be the greatest achiever in the company. In the sports arena and in everyday life are endless competitions to see who will come out on top.

I have also been amazed by the competition and striving in the church, not to serve but to be in a position of authority. Even the apostles saw being first as a goal and argued about who was the greatest (Mark 9:33–34).

However, Jesus turned upside down the world's perception of being first. A person who wants to be first in God's kingdom must be last and live a life of service. We make choices about how we live our lives. We can live according to the world and strive to become the first in all we do, or we can choose to be first in God's kingdom by living a life of humility and service.

Prayer: *Dear God, help us to work for your kingdom by serving others in Jesus' name. Amen*

Thought for the day: How will I serve others today?

Jodi Wheeler (Arizona, US)

PRAYER FOCUS: FOR A SPIRIT OF HUMILITY

God's Nature Never Changes

Read Matthew 22:34–40

A lawyer asked Jesus, 'Which commandment in the law is the greatest?'
Matthew 22:35–36 (NRSV)

Recently, along with my wife and several members of our church, I committed to reading the Bible from beginning to end. As I slogged my way through the Old Testament, I grew weary of the repeated prophecies of God's anger and harsh judgment. I looked with great anticipation toward the love expressed in the New Testament.

Then I asked an important question, 'What made God so angry in the Old Testament?' With that question in mind, I read the Old Testament with more interest and soon discovered at least three major reasons for God's anger: the worship of other gods; injustice to the oppressed, the poor and strangers; and being haughty or self-righteous.

I finally realised that the nature of God revealed in the Old Testament is the same nature as revealed by Christ when he stated that all of the law and the commandments are summed up in the exhortation to love God with all of our heart and to love our neighbour as ourselves. By placing God first, caring for the poor and releasing our pride and self-righteousness, we can begin to live according to God's commandments.

Prayer: *Dear Lord, help us keep you first and foremost in our lives. Open our eyes to new and better ways to help our neighbours, and give us the strength to love as you love. Amen*

Thought for the day: Today I will honour God above all else.

Jeral Williams (Alabama, US)

The Great Conductor

Read Ephesians 4:11–16

The whole body, joined and held together by every supporting ligament, grows and builds itself up in love, as each part does its work

Ephesians 4:16 (NIV)

Recently, I enjoyed a symphony orchestra concert. We arrived early while the musicians were warming up and tuning their instruments. Although we were able to pick out the notes of individual instruments, the sound was a cacophony of disharmonious sounds. However, when the conductor stepped onto the podium and raised his baton to direct the musicians, the result was a blend of perfect tone and harmony. Each selection was executed with appropriate tempo, pitch and dynamics. The result was pleasing to the listeners' ears.

This scene reminded me of all those who belong to the body of Christ. God has given each of us unique gifts—teaching, serving, organising, encouraging and the list goes on. Just as the diverse sounds of the piccolo, violin, drums and tuba each have a part in an orchestra, we each have a part in God's kingdom. We can serve individually. But when we combine our efforts with others' efforts and allow God to direct our paths, the result is a symphony of beautiful works.

Prayer: *Dear Father, thank you for the individual gifts that you give to each of us. Direct us as we work with other believers to create a symphony of good works that is pleasing to you. In Jesus' name we pray. Amen*

Thought for the day: We can use our God-given gifts to work in concert with other believers.

Lu Fullilove (Texas, US)

Citizenship

Read John 3:3–15

Our citizenship is in heaven. And we eagerly await a Saviour from there, the Lord Jesus Christ.
Philippians 3:20 (NIV)

My family and I came to the United States from India in 2006. After five years, we inquired about US citizenship. We learned that we had to pay fees, to have our fingerprints taken and to answer 100 questions in an official interview. My wife and I found it difficult to prepare for the interview because we had no spare time—what with full-time jobs, looking after the house and reading and meditating on the Bible. Only by God's grace did we obtain citizenship.

This experience helped me to see that we are only sojourners on this earth and that our real citizenship is in heaven. For that, we do not have to pay fees because we are invited by God's grace to be citizens of heaven.

In many countries, when children are born they automatically become citizens of the country of their birth. However, to be a citizen of heaven a person need only accept Jesus' invitation—be born again by repentance and confession in the name of Jesus. It is never too late to prepare ourselves for citizenship of heaven.

Prayer: *Holy and righteous heavenly Father, thank you for inviting us to be citizens in your heavenly kingdom. Amen*

Thought for the day: Our most important citizenship is in heaven.

Benjamin D. Christie (Pennsylvania, US)

Time with God

Read Psalm 34:3–10
One does not live by bread alone, but by every word that comes from the mouth of the Lord.
Deuteronomy 8:3 (NRSV)

For a long time my husband and I spent many hours at work. We barely had time to spend together or to share family time to study God's word. But one day while we were reading Ecclesiastes 3:1–5, the scripture passage helped us to decide to make God the centre of our lives. For some time a number of factors, principally work-related, separated us from our Creator. We decided to amend our work schedule and to close our shop earlier at night.

We discovered that a daily encounter with God is crucial to our lives. We know there is time for everything in life, so we must not become careless with our time. Time with God—alone or with family—is essential for our spiritual growth. So now we make the time to speak and to share our thoughts and feelings with the Lord.

Since we learned the importance of spending time with God and reading and studying scripture, our family has been blessed. Thanks be to God!

Prayer: *Dear Lord, help us as we plan our days not to neglect the time we need to spend with you. Amen*

Thought for the day: How can I find more time to spend with God?

Link2Life: *How much time do you spend with God each day?*

Fabiana Vargas de Pfoederl (Misiones, Argentina)

No Unneeded Parts

Read Exodus 31:1–11

I have filled Bezalel with divine spirit, with ability, intelligence and knowledge in every kind of craft.
Exodus 31:3 (NRSV)

Have you ever assembled something and then realised that you have some parts left over? And you just can't seem to work out where that part or piece goes? Your assembled item seems to work properly, so you assume that it wasn't needed in the first place. However, you eventually find out just how important that part was to the whole item. Many things have parts that, even though you can't see them, are still important to the function of that item.

The church is much the same. Some people place a greater value on those positions in the church that are more visible such as the pastor, a teacher or a choir leader. But the truth is, God sees all of us as valuable. In Exodus 31 we see how God filled a craftsman with the skill and ability to work with his hands.

Everyone is valuable to God. Maybe God hasn't called us to preach or teach, but we were each given some ability to serve. We are all enabled by God to do different things. Bezalel's work in building was just as valuable as Moses' work in leading. Even if the work we do isn't seen by a lot of people, it is still valuable.

Prayer: *Loving God, help us to realise that each one of us is important to the work of your Church. In Jesus' name. Amen*

Thought for the day: Everyone has a part and place in the body of Christ.

Terry Sexton (Tennessee, US)

Trespasses

Read Colossians 3:12–14

Blessed are the merciful, for they will be shown mercy.
Matthew 5:7 (NIV)

Years ago I worked in a small office where the employees often had to share work spaces. One day, returning from a few days off, I discovered that someone had been using my desk, had eaten a meal and spilled a drink. I was irritated at the sight of the mess and began cleaning it. Behind me, the radio began broadcasting a daily Bible study with the host inviting listeners to join him in reciting the Lord's Prayer.

Automatically I bowed my head and prayed along, 'Forgive us our trespasses as we forgive those who trespass against us'. I froze in my recitation of the familiar words. I thought, Am I being forgiving? I knew I wasn't. How could I harbour anger and resentment toward one of my colleagues for a trivial offence when the Lord offers me forgiveness for any sin I commit? Ashamed of my petty selfishness, I prayed for God's forgiveness and asked him to bless my colleagues.

Prayer: *Dear Lord, thank you for your promise to forgive us. Remind us of all that you've forgiven us, when we pray, 'Father, hallowed be your name, your kingdom come. Give us each day our daily bread. Forgive us our sins, for we also forgive everyone who sins against us. And lead us not into temptation. Amen.'**

Thought for the day: God has forgiven me; now I can forgive others.

DeVonna R. Allison (Michigan, US)

* Luke 11:2–4 (NIV)

Love Letter from God

Read 2 Timothy 3:10–17

From infancy you have known the Holy Scriptures, which are able to make you wise for salvation through faith in Christ Jesus.
2 Timothy 3:15 (NIV)

A dear friend of mine carries a deep and painful love in her heart. Twenty-five years ago, her eldest son turned his back on her and left home. He has never tried to contact her again, despite repeated attempts on her part to get in touch with him.

This mother's love for her lost son remains inexpressibly deep and true. Each day, she writes in a diary a brief letter to her son, telling him of the daily events in her life. She has already filled three books with these love letters from a mother's aching heart. Perhaps he will one day return, even after she has gone; and he will read her lifetime of love letters to him.

This mother's story reminds me of God's love for his lost children everywhere and his personal love for each of us. The Bible contains God's eternal love letters to us, written a long time ago. When we were lost, we had no desire to read them. But when we return home, they should become the most precious possessions in our lives, to be read and treasured each day.

Prayer: *Loving Father, thank you for the Bible that contains the whole history of your love for us. Amen*

Thought for the day: The Bible is God's love letter to each of us.

Gerald McCann (Gauteng, South Africa)

PRAYER FOCUS: FAMILIES WHO ARE ESTRANGED

The Begat-itudes

Read Matthew 1:1–17

Jesus looked at [the disciples] and said… 'With God all things are possible.'

Matthew 19:26 (NIV)

There they are, all 44 of them—some tall, some short, some Jewish, some Gentile, some righteous, some not—but one thing in particular united them all: they were all in the lineage of Jesus. How can that be? One is even from Moab! One is an adulterer and murderer! And what about that Canaanite prostitute? She's there too.

So what does all this tell us? Surely God can use anyone to accomplish his perfect will. This powerful truth tells me that I do not have to be tall to be useful to God. I do not have to be strong or attractive to be chosen for work in his kingdom. I don't even have to be exceptionally smart. If I trust and obey, God can do anything through me. May we all strive to live for Jesus and not ourselves so that our lives will clearly say, 'My God can do anything through anyone, because he is Lord of all!'

Prayer: *Lord of all, help me to keep my eyes on you and to be obedient. May all your purposes come to pass in my life. Amen*

Thought for the day: Whatever our personal limitations, God can still make use of us.

Robert G. Farmer (Georgia, US)

A Nourishing Gift

Read John 6:48–58

Jesus said, 'I am the bread of life… This is the bread that came down from heaven… the one who eats this bread will live forever.'
John 6:48, 58 (NRSV)

Recently I took in my car for some repairs. Because I didn't know how long the work would take, I had brought along a copy of *El Aposento Alto* (the Spanish edition of *The Upper Room*) to read as I sat in the waiting room. Midway through my reading, I sensed a feeling from the Holy Spirit directing me to give my devotional guide to the receptionist.

I felt a bit disappointed at the Spirit's nudging. It was a brand new issue, and I wanted to finish reading the magazine. Still, I finished the page I was reading before deciding to walk over to the reception desk. As I approached, I noticed a very old issue of *El Aposento Alto* on the desk, the oldest issue I had ever seen. The pages were yellow and torn, and the receptionist was thumbing through them as she had probably done many times before.

I was moved by what I saw and I understood why the Spirit had urged me to give my new copy to the receptionist. I said to her, 'Here is a copy of *El Aposento Alto* for you.' Her eyes opened wide when she saw the magazine, and she said, '*El Aposento Alto*! And it's brand new!' She was extremely enthusiastic in her gratitude for my gift. As for me, I was glad and grateful that I had obeyed God's direction.

Prayer: *Dear God, help us be attuned to your voice and willing to give all that you ask of us. Amen*

Thought for the day: When God nudges us, let us be quick to respond.

Sandra Luz Contreras (Nuevo Leon, Mexico)

Don't Get Too Comfortable

Read Romans 12:9–15

It's necessary for us to pay more attention to what we have heard, or else we may drift away from it.

Hebrews 2:1 (CEB)

The hunt for our first house stretched out for months. My wife and I scoured property magazines and websites. We surfed by, drove by and walked through dozens of potential homes.

The red house had a shimmering newness to it. The rooms echoed with space, the arched doorways dressed up our furniture, and the wood floors reflected the sunlight. But when we brought our first daughter home, those rooms that had seemed so big suddenly shrank. We had become so familiar with our home that the excitement of having found it slowly lost out to thoughts about why it didn't work for us anymore. We lost our sense of wonder about the red house.

As with our house, the events in the Bible—even the miracles—lose the power to impact us if we get too cosy with them. We've read about them and heard sermons about them. But when was the last time we thought about them as actual events? After all, it's not just the story of Jesus' resurrection that makes the difference; it's the reality of that empty tomb.

Prayer: *Dear Lord, never let me take for granted your love for me and your sacrifice in my place. Amen*

Thought for the day: Our life with Christ is new every morning.

John UpChurch (Tennessee, US)

Truly Attractive

Read 1 Samuel 16:1–13

Do not consider his appearance… The Lord does not look at the things people look at… the Lord looks at the heart.
1 Samuel 16:7 (NIV)

The contrast could not have been sharper between the Sunday morning sermon we heard and the television show my daughters and I watched later that afternoon. In the morning, we heard how impressed the prophet Samuel had been by the way Jesse's older sons looked. God, however, searched for qualities that went deeper than outward appearance. The Lord had chosen the youngest son, David, as the future king. While David is described as having 'a fine appearance and handsome features' (v. 12), God was looking for 'a man after his own heart' (see 1 Samuel 13:14).

The television programme, conversely, was about a personal makeover. A woman gets fashion advice, make-up advice and a new hairstyle. By the end of the programme she appears glowingly transformed. It is certainly no sin to take care of one's appearance. For instance, David's great-grandmother, Ruth, washed, perfumed herself and put on her best clothes before going to meet her future husband, Boaz. What really impressed Boaz, though, wasn't her outward appearance but her 'noble character' (see Ruth 3:3–11). The examples of David's family provide a timely reminder to focus on what makes us attractive to God.

Prayer: *Dear Lord, help us to see ourselves and those around us as you do. In Jesus' name we pray. Amen*

Thought for the day: I want my heart to reflect God's love.

Mary van Rheenen (Gelderland, Netherlands)

Snow Angels

Read Romans 5:1–5

Be joyful in hope, patient in affliction, faithful in prayer.
Romans 12:12 (NIV)

As a child growing up in Michigan, I looked forward to snow in winter. I would get bundled up, go out into the crisp cold air, and make snow angels. Then, I would come back into the warm kitchen. The hot cup of chocolate on my cold fingers was comforting. What joy! However, at the age of eight, I was afflicted with polio and could not go out into the cold any more. Many faithful family and friends prayed for me, and I recovered enough to be able to attend church, to graduate from college, to marry, to work for 30 years, to raise two wonderful children and to love and play with my grandchildren.

In recent years, polio has afflicted me with new weakness. When I began to see my strength and stamina diminish, my hope became a flickering candle and patience waned. But I continued to pray faithfully. As I prayed out of my despair—viewing my glass as half empty—I gradually began to feel God's love and to see my glass as half full. It is as if God is telling me, 'I pour out my abundant and lavish love on you and fill your glass full to overflowing so you will not thirst.' Some things—such as tolerating the cold—I cannot do, but now I see clearly what I still can do. I still can love and laugh, worship, praise and pray, sing and serve—and so much more.

Prayer: *Dear God of abundant and lavish love, we pray for your help to be joyful in hope, patient in affliction and faithful in prayer. Amen*

Thought for the day: Prayer is one source of daily spiritual nourishment.

Dwight E. Robeson (Maryland, US)

PRAYER FOCUS: THOSE WHOSE HOPE IS WANING

Steelworker Surprise

Read 1 Peter 2:9–12

You are a chosen race, a royal priesthood, a holy nation, God's own people, in order that you may proclaim the mighty acts of him who called you out of darkness into his marvellous light.
1 Peter 2:9 (NIV)

At high school I excelled in drama, public speaking and English. However, for the last eight years I have worked in a steel-welding shop of 30 employees. A career in steelwork was never in my plans. I've often asked myself, Why am I here? The answer is becoming clear to me. I am the only Christian in my workplace.

I am one of the crew, which has given me the opportunity to talk about spiritual issues with men who rarely even consider them. Many have never attended any church. If my pastor were to try to share the gospel in our canteen, he would be ignored, so perhaps God has placed me there instead.

Each of us spends our day somewhere—whether in an office, at home, on holiday, shopping in a supermarket or working in a loud, dirty steel plant. We might be where God has put us to fulfil a specific purpose or accomplish a special mission.

Prayer: *Dear Jesus, please give us the opportunities and courage to share the gospel. Amen*

Thought for the day: God has a special purpose for each of us.

Daniel Favor (British Columbia, Canada)

Grumpy Gratitude

Read Colossians 1:9–14

Give thanks in all circumstances; for this is God's will for you in Christ Jesus.

1 Thessalonians 5:18 (NIV)

Through the years I've learned that making gratitude lists helps me stay more positive. I use the alphabet, thanking God for something that begins with each letter. Sometimes I thank God for people from the Bible—Abraham, Benjamin, Caleb. Sometimes I use scripture verses alphabetically, such as: 'All have sinned and fall short of the glory of God'; 'Be still, and know that I am God'; 'Create in me a clean heart, O God.'

Recently a friend told me that she makes a 'grumpy gratitude' list in the spirit of 1 Thessalonians 5:18, 'Give thanks in all circumstances.' My friend looks for reasons to be thankful in every situation.

Not long ago I had a door-slamming day. After slamming three or four doors, I remembered my friend's practice and paused to begin a grumpy gratitude list. I thought, 'OK, God, I'm grateful that slammed doors ease frustrations. I'm grateful for doors that keep heat in during the winter and open to let cool breezes in during summer.' My list continued, turning my door-slamming day into a blessing. The grumpy gratitude list helped me recognise how much I had to be thankful for that I had not noticed just moments before.

Even when it appears there is nothing to be grateful for, we can find something for which to thank God.

Prayer: *Whether I am glad or grumpy, God, help me always to be aware of that for which I can be grateful. Amen*

Thought for the day: What's on my 'grumpy gratitude' list today?

Patricia Simmons (Missouri, US)

Grateful for Grace

Read Ephesians 2:1–10

It is by grace you have been saved, through faith—and this not from yourselves, it is a gift of God—not by works, so that no one can boast.
Ephesians 2:8–9 (NIV)

As a court prosecutor, I often review requests to seal the record of someone convicted of a criminal offence. Records are sealed (removed from public access) at the discretion of the court. One question on the form for sealing the record is 'Why is this sealing deserved?' I have only seen one answer that I thought demonstrated true humility. The answer was: 'I don't deserve to have my record sealed, but I would be grateful if the court did grant this request.'

That response is a model of the way we should respond to God's offer of salvation. God, through the death and resurrection of Christ, is willing to erase our entire record of sin if we accept salvation with the right heart. Someone who tries to grasp salvation with good works thinks that he or she has earned and therefore deserves salvation. To think that salvation is a matter of luck or fortune is to see God as arbitrary and therefore to miss the concept of grace. But the person who sees himself or herself as unworthy, yet loved by God, understands that through faith and the grace of God, we are saved from our transgressions. The sealing God provides is not deserved, but we are grateful for his love and Christ's sacrifice that brings salvation.

Prayer: *Dear God, we do not deserve your forgiveness, but humbly submit ourselves to you, asking for your grace. Amen*

Thought for the day: Nothing we do can earn what God gives by grace.

Matthew L. Reger (Ohio, US)

Ready to Share

Read John 21:15–17

Jesus said to Simon Peter, 'Simon son of John, do you love me more than these?' 'Yes, Lord,' he said, 'you know that I love you.' Jesus said, 'Feed my lambs.'

John 21:15 (NIV)

We were visiting churches that support us in our mission ministry. For one meal, our hostess and her husband prepared delicious waffles with a sourdough starter that she had kept for 44 years. It was a present from her husband's aunt and had been in the family for 75 years. Sourdough needs care; it has to be 'fed' regularly with sugar, milk and flour. For the sourdough to stay useful to bake into bread, it has to be tended, used and shared; if not it will 'die'. Our hostess told us that she gave some to a young couple, but it had 'died'. She said: 'Maybe they were not ready to receive the sourdough.'

Since the beginning of time, human beings have been offered many kinds of 'sourdough' from God: our skills, gifts, love and grace. Are we taking good care of them? Are we feeding them so they may feed others? If we don't share our skills and gifts, they will die for lack of use. When we are ready to receive God's love and grace, we can then share with others his greatest gift, Jesus the Christ.

Prayer: *We thank you, Lord, for all the love and grace and forgiveness and peace you have given us. May we always be ready to share these gifts with others. Amen*

Thought for the day: God wants us to feed those who hunger for love and grace.

Eunice Arias (Canelones, Uruguay)

First Things First

Read Matthew 9:1–8

'Be encouraged, my child, your sins are forgiven.'
Matthew 9:2 (CEB)

Like many children, I tried to apply my own sense of order to my life. What was wrong with having at least a taste of dessert before the meat and vegetables? Why couldn't homework come after television time? Fortunately, my mother found even my most compelling arguments less than convincing. Inevitably, her priorities won, and my life has been better as a result.

Jesus also attached great importance to priorities. Before addressing the paralytic's physical maladies, Jesus attended to the man's spiritual illness. Only after healing the sickness of the spirit—'your sins are forgiven'—did Jesus heal the man's physical paralysis. In approaching the situation as he did, Jesus taught a valuable lesson.

Today, time once devoted to setting and attending to priorities is now spent mastering a different approach: multi-tasking. Tasks completed at the same time hardly need an assigned priority. Yet Jesus chose to put spiritual well-being first. I can hear my mother giving a knowing laugh at that idea. 'Like I always said, son, "First things first".'

Prayer: *Thank you, God, for loving reminders of what is important. Amen*

Thought for the day: Matters of the spirit come first.

Robert L. Stephens (Virginia, US)

Hope in Exile

Read Isaiah 52:1–10

Weeping may linger for the night, but joy comes with the morning.
Psalm 30:5 (NRSV)

I could not bring myself to say, 'Merry Christmas'. I knew my friend's Christmas would be overshadowed by concern for her child. As we sang 'O Come, O Come, Emmanuel', about Israel's mourning in exile and crying out to the Lord for deliverance, I was reminded of my friend and her child. Each was held captive in 'lonely exile' from the joy of the Christmas season.

I also thought that while the Church marches through Advent in a month, our personal journeys through Advent may take much longer. When we have a difficult child, a dying spouse, a bout of depression, a crushing disease, a failing marriage, a loss of income or another seismic shift in our lives, we, like Israel, mourn 'in lonely exile', crying out for the Son of God to appear in our lives.

Looking back over unhappy times in my own life, I wondered, Is crying out for the Lord a cry of despair or a cry of hope? Instinctively, I have known that I could not give up hope. Hope carries me through the weeks, months or years of 'lonely exile' and into the peace, love and joy promised in Jesus Christ.

Prayer: *Dear God, grant us courage to hope and to persevere through bleak times in our lives so that we may know the joy you offer. Amen*

Thought for the day: 'Rejoice! Rejoice! Emmanuel shall come to thee, O Israel.'

Cindy Love (Texas, US)

Carrying God's Word

Read Deuteronomy 6:6–9

Oh, how I love your law! It is my meditation all day long.
Psalm 119:97 (NRSV)

Several years ago, someone brought me a Bible from another city. I really loved it because it was small, light and easy to carry with me. However, often after church or a small group meeting, I have forgotten to take my Bible out of my bag so that when I needed it I couldn't immediately remember where it was.

Recently I acquired a new Bible. It is a new translation, and it is large and heavy. Whenever I carry this Bible with me, I am constantly thinking how heavy it is! But at the same time, this new, larger Bible never lets me forget about the word of God.

The Bible in my bag, be it tiny or large, reminds me that following God's word is not always easy. But while it can be difficult to obey God's word, when I read and reflect on it with passion to obey it, my life is filled with the joy and abundance that Jesus promised us.

Prayer: *Heavenly Father, teach us each day to reflect on your word and to do it. As Jesus taught us, we pray, 'Our Father which art in heaven, Hallowed be thy name. Thy kingdom come. Thy will be done, as in heaven, so in earth. Give us day by day our daily bread. And forgive us our sins; for we also forgive every one that is indebted to us. And lead us not into temptation; but deliver us from evil. Amen.'**

Thought for the day: How will I obey the word of God today?

Link2Life: *Give away the Bibles you no longer use.*

Nataliya Konstantinova (Pskov, Russia)

* Luke 11:2–4 (KJV)

The Source of the Gift

Read James 1:17–18

[God's beloved Son] is the image of the invisible God... in him all the fullness of God was pleased to dwell.
Colossians 1:15, 19 (NRSV)

God chose to come to earth in the form of a human baby. How amazing! Instead of coming full-grown and in a dramatic fashion, as a kind of super-hero, God came quietly into the world in the weakest, most vulnerable form—dependent on a human mother for food, protection and loving care. Why did he choose to come to earth as an infant?

If we had been planning the event of God's arrival on earth, we would certainly have taken the super-hero method, with fanfare and drums. Only God would have thought to come as a baby. But again we ask, 'Why?'

God apparently chose to identify with our human condition and to experience life from an earthly perspective, facing temptation, hunger, fatigue, weakness, suffering and death. He humbled himself so that we might discover that his true nature is love. He came to show us how to live and how to love. As God's earthly children, we learn best by following an example; so he sent the best model, the 'perfect gift' in a form that we could understand. How amazing is God's grace!

Prayer: *O God, help us to recognise you in our midst. May we allow you to teach us and to show us the way to fullness of life. Amen*

Thought for the day: God is with us.

Ruth Moorer (New Mexico, US)

Held

Read Matthew 14:25–31
Your constant love, O Lord, held me up.
Psalm 94:18 (GNB)

Dora Greenwell, who lived in 19th-century County Durham in England, was a most remarkable woman. She was self-taught in theology and could read books in a number of other languages. She wrote inspirational verse and devotional prose, and engaged in a wide variety of social concerns, including education, prisons and mental health. All this was done against a daunting background of family difficulties and personal ill-health. In the front of her books is her motto, a cross grasped by a hand and the words: 'Et teneo et teneor—I both hold and am held.'

It is a phrase I learn to appreciate more and more. I try to remember it in all my different daily experiences. However difficult life may be, strength and courage are restored when I remember to hold to the cross and at the same time know that I am held in God's love. Here is our security for this life and the next. Trusting in the cross of Jesus is my sure hope of everything working together for good. Leaning on God is my certainty that I cannot fall from his care.

Prayer: *Lord Jesus Christ, keep my grip on the cross firm as I trust your sure care for me. Amen*

Thought for the day: God holds the cosmos in his care. I cannot fall out of his hands.

Link2 Life: *How can I be a support—a practical, loving hold—for someone today?*

Colin D. Harbach (Cumbria, England)

A Holy Comforter

Read John 14:13–18
Jesus said, 'I will pray the Father, and he shall give you another Comforter, that he may abide with you for ever.'
John 14:16 (KJV)

The farmhouse where I grew up was cold and draughty. I slept upstairs, and the only heat came from a wood stove in the room below. But during the night the fire would go out. My mum worried about my not being warm enough. So on cold nights she would tuck me in, piling on several blankets. Not only did I feel toasty warm, but I also felt safe, loved and comforted. When I think of my childhood those blankets remind me how much I was loved and cared for.

In this passage from the Gospel of John, the Greek word translated 'comforter' is 'parakletos', which also means intercessor, counsellor and advocate. The Comforter Jesus was speaking of is the Holy Spirit that God sends to dwell with us for ever so that we need never feel alone or afraid or insecure or unloved. Once we become adults, we may leave behind childish fears, but when the world caves in and the future appears threatening, we all still need to feel the reassurance that comes when someone comforts us.

Jesus explains that the Comforter will dwell with us and in us. 'I will not leave you comfortless,' he promised (John 14:18). In an often comfortless world, Jesus' words are indeed comforting.

Prayer: *God of all comfort, we thank you for the indwelling of your Holy Spirit. In the name of Jesus we pray. Amen*

Thought for the day: Nothing can separate us from the love of God, which is in Christ Jesus (see Romans 8:38–39).

Jack D. Kendall (Iowa, US)

PRAYER FOCUS: ORPHANS

A Change of Habit

Read Romans 7:14–25
Refresh my heart in Christ.
Philemon 1:20 (NIV)

After deciding to follow Jesus, I am disappointed to find myself still wallowing in habits that are not part of this new life. Despite my best efforts, old tendencies still linger and trip me up. At times I feel stale and discouraged instead of strong and new.

So I was comforted and encouraged to find that Paul struggled with the same issue. He wrote that our human nature can overwhelm our spiritual intentions—to my great sorrow and annoyance. Indeed I know what Paul meant when he said, 'Wretched man that I am!' (Romans 7:24). I sometimes feel as though I'm getting nowhere in my walk with God. My struggle reminds me of trying to log on to a website and continually pressing 'refresh' in the hope that, this time, I might actually get somewhere.

But there is hope for this dilemma. Paul assures us that we are rescued by Jesus. Our heart is refreshed in fellowship—with Jesus and in the presence of other struggling believers. That was the kind of relationship Paul had with Philemon. Keeping hold of scripture and maintaining good fellowship in the church will help us grow out of old habits and into new life.

Prayer: *Thank you, Father God, for knowing our failings and frailties and loving us anyway. Strengthen us by your Spirit to grow in our Christian life with confidence and hope. Amen*

Thought for the day: Spiritual refreshment cures discouragement.

Ann Sloane (New South Wales, Australia)

Learn from the Master

Read Matthew 11:25–30

Jesus said, 'Take my yoke upon you, and learn of me; for I am meek and lowly in heart: and ye shall find rest unto your souls.'

Matthew 11:29 (KJV)

Recently, I attended my first Christian writers' conference in the Blue Ridge Mountains of North Carolina. It was a wonderful experience, meeting other writers and learning from some of the best professionals in the publishing business. Each day we rushed from one lecture to the next, hoping to learn more about our craft. At mealtimes, we had the opportunity to sit at a table with one of the various writers who were speaking at the conference, which provided yet more time to learn.

In most professions, those who are serious about their calling never pass up a chance to learn from the masters of their craft. If we as Christians are serious about our calling, we will never pass up the opportunity to learn from our Master, Jesus Christ. Each day, we will be eager to dine at his table, sharing the Bread of Life.

Just as we writers sought opportunities to talk with other, more experienced writers, Christians have the opportunity to talk with God. We have his written word readily available to us. By spending a little time each day immersed in scripture and setting aside time to talk with God, we can get to know him better and deepen our commitment to follow in the way of Jesus.

Prayer: *Dear God, we pray for your wisdom and guidance that we might be better servants for your kingdom. In Jesus' name we pray. Amen*

Thought for the day: Each of us has an open invitation to sit daily at the Master's feet.

Link2Life: *Can you write a meditation for* The Upper Room?

James P. Willis (Virginia, US)

Travelling

Read Matthew 1:18–25 and Luke 1:28–38

'I am the Lord's servant,' Mary answered. 'May your word to me be fulfilled.'

Luke 1:38 (NIV)

Every summer when I was a child, my family drove from Texas to North Carolina to attend a family reunion. Much of the journey was enjoyably scenic; but the first 550 miles were on an empty desert road. Before we left, my father filled the car with petrol. My mother packed a cool-box full of food and drinks. The children took books, car games and music.

Our summer treks remind me of the incredible journey of Joseph and Mary. I admire them because when they understood that God had a plan for their lives, they got ready. They seriously considered God's vision. They heard the word of God from the angel and took it to heart. Though Joseph and Mary didn't know where the journey would lead, they trusted God.

Sometimes our journey through Advent is scenic and enjoyable, but often it can seem like a long desert trek. In either case, we can help one another to prepare. We can look for God, listen for his call and consider that he has a purpose for us. And, like Mary and Joseph, when we don't quite understand where the journey will lead, we can put our trust in God.

Prayer: *Dear God, thank you for our journey and for church families that are ready and willing to travel with us; in Jesus' name. Amen*

Thought for the day: Trust God for the journey.

Janise McNair (Florida, US)

The Fire Within

Read James 3:2–12

The tongue is a fire, a world of iniquity: so is the tongue among our members, that it defileth the whole body, and setteth on fire the course of nature; and it is set on fire of hell.

James 3:6 (KJV)

This past year, I found myself answering people's questions with snappy words. Every time someone talked to me, I replied with a smart remark, which often resulted in an argument. The harsh words I said started to push me away from the people I cared about most. Tired of the way I was acting, I started to pray, asking God to help.

One night, I opened my Bible at James 3. The idea that the tongue is similar to a fire spoke to me. I reflected on every harsh word I had said and wished that I could rewind my life and change my actions. I found that if I spoke evil of others once, I spoke evil the rest of the day. Like a fire, my harsh words spread. Unfortunately, once the words had come out of my mouth, I couldn't take them back.

Over the past few months, I have learned to think before I speak, making sure that I won't regret what comes out of my mouth. I have learned that when I speak well of those around me, I express God's love within me. Speaking of others in a good way draws me closer to those I care most about and I become more like Christ.

Prayer: *Dear Lord, let the words of my mouth be pleasing to you. Amen*

Thought for the day: Our words can push others away or draw them nearer to God's love.

Lorinda Brenize (Pennsylvania, US)

Through the Best and the Worst

Read 2 Samuel 22:2–7

'In my distress I called to the Lord; I called out to my God. From his temple he heard my voice; my cry came to his ears.'
2 Samuel 22:7 (NIV)

Are they blessings or a series of miracles? My wife Pat and I feel certain about one thing: the events of the past two years of our lives were not coincidences.

We were engaged to be married in December 2009. Two months after our engagement, I decided to move to be closer to Pat in south-east Missouri—three months earlier than I'd originally planned. This move was our first blessing. Two days after my move, Pat was diagnosed with Stage 4 colon cancer and given a one-in-four chance of surviving. She underwent two major surgeries, two minor surgeries, 24 chemo treatments and 29 radiation treatments. Through it all we prayed that God would allow us to enjoy the blessings of life for as long as possible. We are convinced that because of love—the love of God, our pastor, friends, and family—and the amazing work of numerous doctors, Pat's cancerous growths were removed and the cancer was destroyed.

God continues to support us with never-failing love. Even when things don't go as we would like, we know that he loves us still, supporting us through the best and the worst of times.

Prayer: *Gracious God, we give you praise for your love that sustains us through good times and bad. Amen*

Thought for the day: Love is God's healing power.

Kenneth C. Birt (Florida, US)

Holy Conversation

Read 1 Thessalonians 5:12–18

Jesus said, 'Where two or three are gathered in my name, I am there among them.'
Matthew 18:20 (NRSV)

In the evening, when the sun is setting and the tasks of the day are done, I have a sense of joyful anticipation. I await a phone call from my sister in Christ, Olga, and we begin our daily evening prayer on the telephone.

When I became a believer, I could not see the point of prayer. Why pray, I thought, if God is all-knowing and knows our thoughts before we do? God will do what is best. I reasoned that I am only human and may ask for the wrong thing.

Gradually, however, I began to feel the need to pray. And when I was able to pray with another person, prayer became a necessity. I stopped asking myself why I should pray to an all-knowing God. I simply needed that evening conversation with the Lord.

Olga and I have been praying together for five years now. Our friends and family know about our prayer time and often ask us to pray for one situation or another. And we do pray, understanding that God has given us the privilege to address ourselves directly to him. Jesus said, 'Where two or three are gathered in my name, I am there among them.'

Prayer: *Dear Lord, thank you that we can always converse with you through prayer. Amen*

Thought for the day: Prayer is a much-needed conversation with God.

Galina Samson (Voronezh, Russia)

Lift Your Eyes

Read Romans 5:6–11
While we were God's enemies, we were reconciled to him through the death of his Son.
Romans 5:10 (NIV)

Recently, after my five-year-old niece had been told not to swing from the branches of a very small tree, we heard a loud crack as she and the branch fell. My niece timidly walked to her dad, hanging her head as she pointed to the broken branch. My brother bent down, spoke something to her and they hugged. In no time, she was again laughing and playing.

As God's child, I can easily picture hanging my head low when I know I've broken one of his commands. But that day, I saw the situation from a different angle. My niece disobeyed, was powerless to remedy her situation and was too ashamed to look her father in the eye. But he reached down to meet her where she was. Stretching out his hand, he lifted her eyes to meet his where she could see his desire to forgive and restore their relationship.

It's the same for us. Covered in sin and shame, we are powerless to reach a holy God. Our heavenly Father must reach down to us. So God sent Jesus Christ, who stretched out his hands on the cross, beckoning us to lift our eyes and remember that God desires to forgive and restore us.

Prayer: *Holy God, when we sin, lift our eyes to the cross so that we can embrace your forgiveness and the power to live as your beloved children. Amen*

Thought for the day: We have a Father in heaven whose greatest desire is reconciliation with us.

Shadia Hrichi (California, US)

God With Us

Read Isaiah 9:2–7
God said, 'I will never leave you or abandon you.'
Hebrews 13:5 (CEB)

At Christmas, we hear secular songs or television adverts that refer to this time of year as being magical or a time for miracles. Even when the world seems to try to remove Christ from Christmas, there is something special about this time of the year.

But just what is it that makes Christmas so special? Our desire for goodwill and peace is only a small part. Christmas is special for one important reason: God came in the form of a child, became like us and became one of us, while still remaining divine.

'God is with us.' What a wonderful promise! But the really good news is that this promise extends beyond the few weeks of the Christmas season. For believers, this promise sustains us every day of our lives. As children of God, we know that he is with us for ever. That's the great news: God is with us. 'God so loved the world that he gave his one and only Son' (John 3:16, NIV)—to save us.

So as we go about managing all the responsibilities of this busy time of the year, let's devote some time each day to remember the wonderful promise of Emmanuel: God is with us for ever.

Prayer: *Dear God, thank you for your great promise never to leave us. Amen*

Thought for the day: The real gift of Christmas is God's presence with us.

Anthony Marinez (New York, US)

God Hears Every Prayer

Read James 5:15–18

Lord, you have examined me. You know me. You know when I sit down and when I stand up. Even from far away, you comprehend my plans.
Psalm 139:1–2 (CEB)

At times, I begin my daily prayers reluctantly because I feel that I am endlessly whining about my struggles and issues, which are insignificant compared to what others around the world are going through. Yet, I still seek God in prayer. As small as my issues may be, they are too much for me to carry alone. Some mornings I begin my daily prayers, saying, 'Here I am again, Lord.' Then I pray, 'God, I know you have things to deal with that are bigger than my little stuff.'

The reality is that God does care about the little things that happen in our daily lives. We are all God's children, and he loves and cares for each of us. I am so thankful that we serve a God who does not compare one person's struggles to another's, but is big enough to handle them all.

Prayer: *Most gracious God, thank you for affirming us as your children and for reminding us that you care about even the smallest issues in our lives. Amen*

Thought for the day: Bring all your concerns to the Lord.

Shawana A. Brown (Tennessee, US)

Waiting

Read Isaiah 40:3–5

This is the one of whom the prophet Isaiah spoke when he said, 'The voice of one crying out in the wilderness: "Prepare the way of the Lord, make his paths straight." '
Matthew 3:3 (NRSV)

My two-year-old grandson, Emilio, and I were watching for his mother to return from the university. As on every evening, we stationed ourselves by the window that allowed us to see the gate to our home. When I saw her, I said to Emilio, 'Your mother is here.' With all the joy and excitement of a two-year-old, he shouted, 'She's here! She's here!' as he went to the door to greet her with hugs and kisses.

My experience with Emilio reminds me of the season of Advent, which is a season of waiting. The church awaits the coming of the Christ-child. The season of Advent invites us to prepare for his coming. The Anointed One came over 2,000 years ago, but each year we await his return. Are we prepared to receive him? Do we, like Emilio, wait eagerly for the Beloved One to knock at our door? May the coming of the Lord find us prepared to receive him!

Prayer: *God of all seasons, thank you for the blessing of a time to wait for your Son, our Lord and Saviour, in whose name we pray. Amen*

Thought for the day: Christ will come again. Are we prepared?

Luis P. Hidalgo Ruiz (Araucania, Chile)

The Way

Read John 14:1–6

Jesus answered [Thomas], 'I am the way, the truth, and the life. No one comes to the Father except through me.'

John 14:6 (CEB)

I have problems finding my way. When I embark on any trip I frequently get lost and require detailed directions. I rely heavily on a sat-nav to help me get where I want to go.

In these wonderful verses from John's Gospel, Jesus is telling his disciples of his final destination. It is an amazing place with room for all. When Thomas wants directions and a map, our Lord firmly states that the only route to our heavenly destination is through him: 'I am the Way, the Truth and the Life' (John 14:6).

These verses from John were my dear grandfather's favourites. As a retired pastor, he quoted many scripture verses but none with the passion and fire that he recited these verses from John. Although he often read them on sad occasions—at the deathbed of his brother and at the funerals of many loved ones—my grandfather saw them as joyful words.

When we give ourselves to Jesus Christ, he gives us directions to that special place. We even have a guide—God's word. We have no further need for a map or a sat-nav. What a wonderful feeling to know that we are never travelling alone and that our Saviour has prepared the way!

Prayer: *Our gracious Guide, continue to lead us and direct us in your service. We give you thanks for preparing the way for us. Amen*

Thought for the day: Where is the Lord directing me today?

Sheila Hester (North Carolina, US)

A Tender Salvation

Read Psalm 121:1–8

The Lord will keep you from all evil; he will keep your life.
Psalm 121:7 (NRSV)

One day a bird flew into our living-room through an open door and was unable to find its way out. It became very frustrated and bumped against the ceiling until its head began to bleed. Finally, it stopped and perched on the curtain rail. My daughter slowly reached out with her hand and gently grasped the little bird. The bird then allowed my daughter to set it free.

Similarly, God watches us when we rush into obstacles in life. These hardships, bad choices and mistakes can cause damage and pain to our souls. In the midst of anguish and distress, we may not always feel the tender hand of our Creator who watches over us and helps us in the right moment. But if we have the wisdom to allow God gently to hold and guide us, our soul can be calmed as we experience his power and love.

Prayer: *Thank you, God, for loving us. Thank you for your willingness always to help us and to calm our fears. We pray as Jesus taught us, saying, 'Our Father which art in heaven, Hallowed be thy name. Thy kingdom come. Thy will be done in earth, as it is in heaven. Give us this day our daily bread. And forgive us our debts, as we forgive our debtors. And lead us not into temptation, but deliver us from evil: For thine is the kingdom, and the power, and the glory, for ever. Amen.'*

Thought for the day: God's gentle hand reaches toward us every day.

Bozhidarka Ivanova (Varna, Bulgaria)

PRAYER FOCUS: THOSE FEELING TRAPPED
* Matthew 6:9–13 (KJV)

Willing to Serve?

Read Colossians 3:20–24

Whatever your task, put yourselves into it, as done for the Lord and not for your masters.
Colossians 3:23 (NRSV)

Stephanie, our church's youth director, asked me to accompany her and the teenagers on a week-long mission trip. I had a laundry list of reasons why I was the wrong person to go, and so I replied unenthusiastically, 'I'll pray about it.' Stephanie seemed convinced that I was going to join them. I wasn't so sure.

At work, I teach primary-age children, and I wasn't sure about living and working with teenagers for a whole week. We would be doing repairs on houses and garden work; tools were not my forte. Also, I would be driving to sites all around the city, and we could get lost. A simple trip would require packing up our whole crew, tools included, and travelling together to a different location. Yet, when I prayed about my concerns, I sensed a real peace from God. Eventually, I consented to go on the trip.

The mission trip turned out to be the most meaningful, well-spent week of my entire year. Most of what I feared did not materialise. And I learned that if we are willing to serve, God will put us to work. He knows what basic qualifications are needed for us to serve effectively: our willingness and our faith.

Prayer: *Dear Lord, help us to be willing vessels to serve you in whatever capacity you choose. Amen*

Thought for the day: How can I serve as God's hands and feet for someone today?

Lin Daniels (Massachusetts, US)

Hope in the Arms of Jesus

Read Mark 10:13–16

[Jesus] took the children in his arms, put his hands on them and blessed them.

Mark 10:16 (NIV)

It was during the Advent season, a time that as a people of faith we joyfully prepare our hearts for the coming of the Christ child, and I had been asked to conduct the funeral for a two-year-old child. In this time of joy and anticipation for so many, this family and their close friends were experiencing heartbreak as they mourned a beloved child.

The message I focused on during that service was from the Gospel of Mark, where the little children came to Jesus. I find comfort and assurance in knowing that just as Jesus received that two-year-old child into his eternal care, he takes all of us into his arms.

In the midst of sadness and loss, we can take comfort and find hope in knowing that Jesus is a constant companion to us all, even when we grieve. Christ is with us; we are never alone. He lifts us into his arms, and we are blessed.

Prayer: *Dear Jesus, even when times of sadness or loss occur, we draw assurance that you care for us. Keep us all in your loving arms. Amen*

Thought for the day: In all situations, Christ offers hope.

Jerry W. Krueger (Texas, US)

PRAYER FOCUS: FAMILIES GRIEVING THE DEATH OF A CHILD

Questioning God

Read Isaiah 64:1–4

If only you would tear open the heavens and come down!
Isaiah 64:1 (CEB)

Many of us can relate to what the prophet Isaiah must have been feeling when he uttered the words above, even if we aren't audacious enough to speak them. At times, we want God to come down to earth with real power to shake up the world and to make things right. In the same way, we are sometimes tempted to put our faith in economic, political or military power, hoping that by sheer force we can make the world right—or at least make things right for our lives, our families and our nation. The prophet captures the down-to-earth longing in many human hearts.

Advent teaches us that God does not come with power to make the world right. He comes down from heaven, and hope for a new world is born in a nondescript cow stall in an obscure town called Bethlehem. God arrives by way of the human sweat and blood by which everyone is born. He comes down to save the world, not by what the world calls power, but by the subversive and often hidden power of self-giving love.

God comes down, and hope is born. But we miss it if we aren't looking in the right place. This Advent let us train our eyes, minds and hearts so we will be ready for hope to be born in each of us.

Prayer: *Dear God, give us eyes to see your power in the self-giving love of Jesus Christ. Amen*

Thought for the day: God comes down, and hope is born among us.

James Harnish (Florida, US)

Don't Miss This Banquet!

Read John 6:35–40

Do not work for food that spoils, but for food that endures to eternal life, which the Son of Man will give you.
John 6:27 (NIV)

Every spring the farmer who owns the field next to our home spends several days planting seeds. When he leaves, hundreds of honking geese fly in and start eating. I imagine them saying, 'Tell all the geese to come. This banquet is too good to miss. Here's our opportunity to stuff ourselves.' We love to watch them crowd together and then eat and eat. It's amazing that any seeds survive, but the farmer still has a good harvest in the autumn.

Jesus also calls people everywhere to come to his banquet. He doesn't want anyone to be left behind or unaware of the awesome opportunities and privileges that come to those who love and follow him. We should be more excited than the geese and eager to tell our family, friends, acquaintances and even strangers about his promises and love. As we pray about opportunities to share this good news, God will give us the wisdom and opportunities to share.

Prayer: *Thank you, God, that we can come to you for unlimited spiritual bread and water. We want to know and to experience your promises and love. Amen*

Thought for the day: The good news is meant to be shared.

Link2Life: *With whom can you share the good news today?*

Donna H. Eliason (Washington, US)

Close to Jesus

Read Hebrews 4:14–16
Come near to God and he will come near to you.
James 4:8 (NIV)

I have a wonderful nativity set crafted in beige and brown ceramics that I put on display during the Christmas season. It sits on a table at the perfect height for my youngest niece, Grace, to reach the figures. Each time she visits I notice that all the figures have been pushed up close to the baby. All are touching each other, and many of the animals' noses touch the manger as they look at the Christ child.

Grace's instinct is to place everyone close to Jesus. I, on the other hand, place each figure at an artistic distance from that central character. This last time, as I looked at the distance I place between the figures, I asked myself, 'Am I placing distance between God and me? Why do I shy away?' Little children never seemed to have a problem running to Jesus. He never turned them away. And so today I come as a little child. I'm peeping over the edge and looking into the hope that lies before me: an approachable, incarnate God—Jesus Christ, humble and able to save.

Prayer: *Great and glorious Lord God, help me to remember that you are also a tender Father who sent Jesus Christ to earth to demonstrate that tenderness and love to us. Amen*

Thought for the day: Today I will draw close to Jesus.

Linda Barrett (Alabama, US)

Passionate Noise

Read Matthew 9:35–38

These are not drunk, as you suppose, for it is only nine o'clock in the morning.
Acts 2:15 (NRSV)

A colleague invited me to a function about a business opportunity. Though I went, the event held nothing of interest for me. And to make matters worse, the room was filled with deafening noise from presenters and attendees. But, determined not to disappoint my host, I looked for something I could enjoy about the evening. Suddenly, the noise in the room that so closely resembled a bar full of drunken revellers reminded me of Peter's words in Acts 2:15: 'These are not drunk, as you suppose, for it is only nine o'clock in the morning.' The noise grew from people's enthusiasm.

The memory of Peter's sermon enabled me to enjoy the rest of the event. Watching the passion with which the speakers delivered their messages about the opportunities to earn extra income, I no longer saw the participants as only a noisy throng. Instead I wondered about the impact I could have for God's kingdom if I pursued my Christian calling with the same vigour!

This is what God calls all believers to do—to venture out into the harvest with courage and exuberant commitment to tell others the Good News.

Prayer: *Almighty God, thank you for your loving care and concern for us. Give us passion and enthusiasm to venture into your world fearlessly to seek and love those who do not know you. Amen*

Thought for the day: How passionate am I about sharing my faith in Christ?

Philip Polo (Nairobi, Kenya)

Pain and Joy

Read Isaiah 61:1–4

May the God of hope fill you with all joy and peace in believing.
Romans 15:13 (NRSV)

I remember my mother's last Christmas Eve. I spent the day with her in her hospital room; and after the carol service at night, friends accompanied me to the hospital. One person took his guitar, and we sang 'Silent night, holy night'. My mother, who had not spoken in days, began to sing softly and clearly, 'all is calm, all is bright'. Stunned and overwhelmed, we continued, singing 'Joy to the world'. I remember the peace on my mother's face as we gathered around her hospital bed and sang songs about the coming of our Lord and God.

Christmas joy is not a given for those who mourn the loss of a parent, child, sibling or good friend. Looking at an empty place at the table brings unimaginable pain. Pain is deep and not always fleeting. However, believing and understanding the meaning of Advent may bring joy in the midst of despair. The pain rooted in suffering will come, as it should; but so will joy. I find joy in the coming of Christ even as I look at the space on the sofa where my mother sat every Christmas Day.

Joy came to us in the birth of an infant, and joy will return to us in glory. During Advent, we celebrate the incarnation of Jesus, the promised return of the risen Christ in final glory, and the perpetual presence of Christ in our lives.

Prayer: *Praise God, that when we mourn, we will be comforted and that pain will turn to glorious joy in Jesus Christ our Lord. Amen*

Thought for the day: Today I will celebrate the presence of Christ in my life.

Melanie Gordon (Tennessee, US)

Jesus Makes the Difference

Read Colossians 1:15–20

The Word became flesh and made his dwelling among us. We have seen his glory, the glory of the one and only Son, who came from the Father, full of grace and truth.

John 1:14 (NIV)

Years ago, I heard someone say that Jesus is the window through which we see God. Even though Jesus came to live among us as a person and was in some ways just like us, he also embodied all the qualities of God.

During Advent, we reflect on what Jesus has meant to the world since the time of his birth. The more we learn of Jesus, the more we learn of God. God loved the world and sent Jesus so that we would experience new life through him.

On Christmas Day, when I was a child, we set an extra place at the table for Jesus. My mum baked a cake in honour of his birth. Santa Claus, Christmas trees and gifts were part of our Christmas tradition; but we had no doubt that Christmas was about Jesus.

This Christmas season, let us stop to consider the difference Jesus has made in history and in individuals' lives. Thinking of him as the window through which we see God may make a huge difference in the way we celebrate Christmas.

Prayer: *Dear God, thank you for the gift of Jesus Christ, for all he has done for us and all he has enabled us to do through his love and grace. May we believe with heart and mind that Jesus shows us the way to you. Amen*

Thought for the day: Jesus is the window through which we see God.

Troy Holloway (Florida, US)

PRAYER FOCUS: TO SEE GOD MORE CLEARLY

The Women of Christmas

Read Luke 1:39–48, 56; 2:22–38

Mary said… 'From now on all generations will call me blessed, for the Mighty One has done great things for me.'
Luke 1:46–49 (NIV)

As a widow, I struggle after the holidays. The family has been together, and I have stayed up too late and entertained too much. Now I have to go back to work, and the aura of festivity is overtaken by Kentucky's grey skies. Yet when I read through the Christmas stories again, I find my spirit renewed.

In particular, I am struck by the bravery and joy of the women of the Christmas narrative. Upright and devout, Elizabeth had spent a lifetime longing for a child, perhaps wondering if God had forgotten her. Mary, a young girl full of the excitement of new birth and the dedication of her first-born son, was taken aback by Simeon's declaration that a sword would pierce her heart. Anna the prophetess, whose marriage ended in her husband's death after only seven years, had spent the rest of her life serving God in the temple at Jerusalem. And one day, when she was very old, she saw Jesus.

These women were the first to *really* know—first-hand—about the birth of a Saviour. These women declared God's goodness and authority though each had endured the agony of unfulfilled dreams. What examples they are for us in this season! They overcame incredible grief and received the best gift of all.

Prayer: *Heavenly Father, this holiday season, draw near to those who are lonely and fill them with your kindness. In our Saviour's name. Amen*

Thought for the day: God sends hope into our unfulfilled dreams.

Linda Jeffrey (Kentucky, US)

Looking Ahead

Read 1 Kings 3:3–15

Teach us to number our days, that we may gain a heart of wisdom.
Psalm 90:12 (NIV)

During the last week of every December, many magazines and television shows devote special editions to reviewing the past year. I do the same. Before I throw my old calendar away, I look back through the months of scribbled appointments and activities. This helps me reflect on the events of my personal and spiritual life.

When I put up my new calendar, I wonder what I need to do differently to make this a better year and to be a better Christian. This reminds me of the passage in 1 Kings when God asked Solomon, the newly crowned king, what gift he would like from the Almighty. Solomon realised that he lacked maturity and needed help in ruling a kingdom. Rather than wealth, long life or revenge against his enemies, Solomon asked God for wisdom. God was pleased and gave him the wisdom he needed to lead his people.

Our Creator has already given each of us gifts. As I look ahead to the new year, I pray for wisdom to recognise my gifts and to seek opportunities to use them in God's service. I hope that when I look through the calendar this time next year, the dates will be filled with scribbled notations of days spent serving God.

Prayer: *God of all times, give us wisdom to serve in your kingdom. Teach us to love others as you love us. Amen*

Thought for the day: This year I resolve to use my gifts to serve God.

Terry Cobb (Missouri, US)

We Serve the Lord

Read Luke 24:13–32

Joshua said, 'As for me and my household, we will serve the Lord.'
Joshua 24:15 (NRSV)

For many years as a family, my wife and I did not pray at meals. But as we have grown older, our faith has grown deeper. So when we had grandchildren, we decided that the best thing we could give them and their parents is a good example. So now we give not only food and fellowship at the table; we give glory to God for all he gives us. As Joshua said to the people of Israel, 'As for me and my household, we will serve the Lord' (Joshua 24:15, NIV).

Jesus was recognised for who he was as he shared a meal with two of his followers he had met on the road to Emmaus. When Jesus broke the bread and gave thanks, their eyes were opened; they knew who Jesus was. At our table I also want to reflect who I am in my faith and give thanks to the Lord. Now, when the table is set, as we serve the food we also serve the Lord.

Prayer: *O God, may we thirst and hunger as much for your holy word as we do for the food and drink that is before us. We give thanks for your natural and spiritual blessings. Amen*

Thought for the day: There is no better time than now to serve the Lord.

Jim M. Quint (Kansas, US)

A Real Resolution

Read Matthew 5:13–16

Let your light shine before others, so that they may see your good works and give glory to your Father in heaven.
Matthew 5:16 (NRSV)

In the Sermon on the Mount (Matthew 5:3—7:27), Jesus was giving the disciples their purpose here on earth, instructing them in spreading the message of salvation and eternal life. When Jesus said, 'You are the salt of the earth [and]... the light of the world' (Matthew 5:13–14), he was calling us to make a positive difference in the world. Salt adds flavour and preserves food. Light dispels the darkness, so that we can instantly see the way ahead. In a similar way, we can add flavour to the lives of others just by being encouragers. By sharing the message of salvation, we can shine light into dark situations.

As we come to the end of the year we start thinking about New Year's resolutions, about making a decision to mend something, change something or resolve something. What if this year we resolve to follow the Sermon on the Mount? Telling others about Jesus can be difficult—especially in today's world. We often fear rejection, mockery and even persecution. But if we resolve to let Christ live through us, we can be the salt and light of the earth. We can make a difference in our homes, our families, our workplaces and our communities.

Prayer: *Dear God, give us the courage to stand for you in the face of mockery or persecution. Give us opportunities to help spread the good news, and to see lives changed. Amen*

Thought for the day: With God's help, I can make a difference in someone's life today.

Vince Beaver (Ohio, US)

God Leads Us Still

Read Psalm 46:1–11

Be still, and know that I am God! I am exalted among the nations, I am exalted in the earth.
Psalm 46:10 (NRSV)

When my wife was in the intensive care unit, everyone told me to have faith that she would get well. But I had my doubts. My father had recently died, even though I had placed my faith in God, trusting that my father would survive.

If my wife were to die, it would be a profound loss for me and my family. To compound our fears, our medical insurance was running out. The ensuing weeks saw my wife on the verge of death.

In my desperation, I found the verse from Psalm 46 above. Even if I could not have faith in the outcome, I found I could have confidence that whatever happened, God would be in the midst of it all.

The long-term effects of my wife's hospital stay made her recuperation slow, and my emotional health was wounded by the crisis. Even so, not once did I feel abandoned by God. He was there through the support of our church; he was there to provide our family nourishment; he was there to help our financial needs.

Today I feel at peace. Psalm 46 showed me how to be still and to trust God to heal the wounds of body and spirit and to restore life and faith.

Prayer: *Dear Lord, through the stormy and dark paths of life, you are our sure guide, who leads us to a place of quiet solitude and the peace that passes all understanding (Philippians 4:7). Thank you. Amen*

Thought for the day: When troubles come, be still and wait for God.

Abelardo Flores Zertuche (Nuevo Leon, Mexico)

Take the Step

Read Matthew 14:22–33
Peter got out of the boat, started walking on the water, and came toward Jesus.
Matthew 14:29 (NRSV)

Most of us are familiar with the scene depicted in the Bible passage above. We may have read or heard it many times, but usually our focus is on how Peter became afraid and started sinking. Today, I was introduced to another perspective. We know that Peter became overwhelmed with fear; we all can identify with that experience. But how many of us can identify with Peter's first action: taking a step?

Taking that first step required courage, faith and risk. Sometimes we may feel as if we're in a storm with raging circumstances surrounding us. We know God is there, but sometimes we're too afraid to leave the comfort of our boat to follow him. What if we choose to be like Peter and take a step? We may be afraid, but we can find comfort when we pray and hear God's response: 'Take heart, it is I; do not be afraid.'

We may step out and meet a flood of obstacles. But just as Peter was rescued, God will be there with an extended hand to save us as well. We can trust God, take that step and never look back. We will soon discover that one step can change the course of our entire life.

Prayer: *Mighty God, help us to take that first step toward you. Let us experience your love and grace as we walk in relationship with you each day. In Jesus' name we pray. Amen*

Thought for the day: Like Peter, I can trust God and step out of my boat.

Clara Lilly (South Carolina, US)

Small Group Questions

Wednesday 4 September

1. Read Deuteronomy 14:22–28. In this passage, what is the purpose of the tithe? How are tithes used in the community? How does this passage change or support your understanding of tithing?

2. Who or what has shaped your feelings about tithing?

3. Do you think that Luke 6:28 (today's quoted Bible verse) should be taken literally? What do you think 'Give, and it will be given to you', means in a practical sense?

4. Today's author suggests that we can tithe our time as well as our money. Is this idea new to you? Do you think Ruth's idea of devoting an average of 2.4 hours of time every day to serving God is realistic?

5. Name some ways you already contribute toward 'tithing your time'. Did Ruth's list bring other ideas for giving of your time to mind?

6. Is it easier for you to tithe money or time? Why?

7. Does this meditation change your view about how you use your time? Are there specific actions you might take as a result?

Wednesday 11 September

1. When you pray the words, 'Your kingdom come, your will be done on earth as it is in heaven', what situations or circumstances come to your mind? Do those situations usually point to the actions of others, or to your own behaviour?

2. What responsibility do you feel to take part in God's will being done? In your experience, is doing God's will more about doing what's right or about correcting what's wrong in the world? Think of some occasions when you struggle to do God's will personally, and some where you see the need for God's influence to be more present in the world.

3. Describe your earliest memory of praying the Lord's Prayer. Who taught you to pray this prayer?

4. Which phrase of the Lord's Prayer has the most meaning for you? Why?

5. When and where do you pray the Lord's Prayer? Do you pray this prayer in your personal prayer time or only in formal worship? Is the Lord's Prayer a meaningful prayer for you? Why or why not?

6. If you were to pray the Lord's Prayer with, 'Your kingdom come, your will be done in me, or through me, as it is in heaven', what actions on your part does that bring to mind?

Wednesday 18 September

1. Have you ever felt hungry for God's word? What were the circumstances in your life when you felt that hunger? How did you go about satisfying that hunger? Did you satisfy your hunger on your own or with others?

2. Think about your life as a Christian over time. Do you hunger for God's word more or less than when you were a new Christian? Have there been other times in the course of your life as a Christian that you have felt especially hungry for God's word? Why do you think that is?

3. Which books of the Bible provide you with the best spiritual nourishment? Why? Are there particular parts of the Bible that you have been drawn to in particular circumstances? For example, what part of the Bible do you turn to if you feel discouraged? Joyful? In need of inspiration? Dealing with a difficult problem?

4. How does your church encourage you to read the Bible? What Bible study groups or study programmes have you heard about or participated in?

5. How have you experienced the Bible contributing to your growth/ maturing as a Christian? Try to remember specific instances in which reading the Bible helped you become a more faithful disciple.

6. Think about how regular encounters with the Bible might fit in to your plan for being a healthy follower of Christ.

Wednesday 25 September

1. What does the Bible have to say about how we are to show 'hospitality' to others? Is hospitality to be practised for hospitality's sake, or is there always an underlying motive? What are the hoped for outcomes to practising hospitality? What are some consequences if we fail to show hospitality to others?

2. Recall a time when you were the recipient of hospitality. How did it feel to be welcomed as a guest? How did you respond to the offer of hospitality?

3. How do you show hospitality in your home? In your community? In your church?

4. Different cultures show hospitality in different ways. Have you ever experienced the hospitality of someone from a different culture? What did you learn from the experience? How did this experience help you to understand hospitality differently?

5. What do you think of this method of evangelism? Could/would you participate in this way—as a missionary? How might you respond to someone who wants to share their religious beliefs with you, especially if their beliefs differ from yours?

6. Who do you think of when you hear the word 'hospitality'? Describe that person and what it is about their behaviour that strikes you as hospitable.

7. How high a priority do you give the ministry of hospitality in your own life? Why? When do you have opportunities to practise hospitality?

Wednesday 2 October

1. How hard is it for you to relinquish control? Does the degree differ with the situation/circumstances? Describe a time when you gave up control of a situation. How difficult was it to not be in control? Why was it difficult? What surprised you about the experience?

2. Why do you think we fear losing control? Why is giving up control sometimes a good thing? In what aspect or concern in your life would you like to give up control? Why?

3. In Luke 22:42 Jesus releases control to God praying, 'Not my will but yours be done.' When have you prayed a prayer like this? What happened when you gave control to God?

4. What do you consider to be your 'greatest need'? How is that need being met? If your need is not being met, what could change the situation/circumstance?

5. How has your community of faith relied on God to lead your congregation in some ministry or mission? When has your congregation resisted God's leading in a decision or action? What was the outcome?

6. Consider today's quoted scripture. How can we—as individuals—know we are being led by the Spirit of God?

Wednesday 9 October

1. Do you prefer to pray alone or in community? Why? What experiences have shaped this preference?

2. What might be special about having a 'prayer partner'? How would praying with someone else/others be different from praying alone?

3. Have you ever made a commitment to pray for someone or some situation? What helped you keep that commitment to pray?

4. What does Romans 8:26–27 mean to you personally? How does/could this apply to your relationship with God?

5. Describe a time you felt deeply connected to God during prayer. What were you praying about? How did you feel God's presence with you?

6. When do you pray? How do you make time for prayer throughout the day? What situations remind you to pray?

7. When you pray, does an image of God come to mind? If so, what is it? Do you ever imagine the Holy Spirit in your mind's eye, interceding for you? If so, what is the sense you have of God's Spirit?

8. If you have never done it before, would you consider committing to prayer together with someone on a regular basis for a month or two? Can you think of a person you might feel comfortable praying with?

Wednesday 16 October

1. What 'wobbles' do you see in your own spiritual life? What can you do to repair those wobbles?

2. What does 'holy living' mean for you? How can you pursue holy living in routine, everyday life?

3. How has your church community supported your spiritual disciplines? Who has modelled holy living for you? What have you learned about holy living from these spiritual role models?

4. What do you think the early church knew about the value of spiritual disciplines that the church today may have forgotten or simply disregards?

5. If you ever neglect a 'spoke' of the spiritual disciplines, which one is it: prayer, fasting, meditation, reading scripture, worship, confession, solitude or study? Why do you think this is so?

6. What for you is the most important aspect of your spiritual life? How or through what means do you maintain your spiritual life?

7. Describe a time when you felt a need for more spiritual discipline in your life. What did you do? Who did you turn to for help or support?

8. How might our failure to 'pursue the things of God' influence/affect our relationship with others?

Wednesday 23 October

1. Considering your own typical life pattern or routine, where do you 'live' most of the time—in the past, present, or future? Which of these is the most pleasant for you? Which would you more prefer to avoid or forget? Why? Are you satisfied with the way you prioritise these three? Why or why not?

2. To what might you be devoting too much time in your daily life? Where would you be wise to devote more time? What keeps you from making a change?

3. What do you think is required to 'live in the present'? Why is it important to live in the present?

4. Read Esther 4:14. When have you felt that God has led you to a particular moment for a specific purpose? How did you feel in that moment? How did you discern God's purpose for you in that moment?

5. What prayer practices or spiritual disciplines help you to be present in the moment? What new prayer practice or spiritual discipline would you like to try?

6. What is your reaction to Nicola's host's response in paragraph one? Was it in any way tempered by Nicola's insight in paragraph two?

Wednesday 30 October

1. What do you think about using a structured prayer method? Would you ever consider using the ABC prayer method? Why or why not?

2. When your sleep is interrupted, or your mind is troubled, do you think of that as an invitation to pray? When do you feel most prompted to pray? Do you find prayer to be a settling or relaxing experience?

3. If you've heard of other prayer methods, describe one or two. Which do you think would be most effective?

4. What are you thankful for today? Who has been on your mind today? Who needs healing? What parts of the world need God's loving presence?

5. When do you pray? Why do you pray? How does your prayer practice shape your daily life?

6. Describe a powerful prayer experience you have had. Who was praying and what were they praying for? What made that prayer so powerful? How can you help others to have similar prayer experiences?

Wednesday 6 November

1. Boe's dress is a physical reminder of the prayers she is dancing. Do you use physical objects or reminders when you pray? Why or why not? What physical objects help you enter a prayerful frame of mind?

2. Describe a meaningful prayer service you have attended. Who was present? What kinds of prayers were spoken? What made the service meaningful for you?

3. Do you agree or disagree with the statement: 'any act done in love on behalf of another is a kind of prayer'? What daily acts of love might you include in your prayer practice?

4. Reflect on the faith traditions that have come to you from your ancestors. Do you know their origins? From whom did you learn them?

5. How do you pass along your faith traditions to the next generations? How can your church support and instruct young people in the ways of faith and prayer?

6. Whom or what do you want to pray for today? Share your prayer concerns among the group, and pray for one another this week.

Wednesday 13 November

1. When have you most wanted to be first? When have you achieved the goal of being first? How did you achieve it? How did it feel to be the first? What surprised you about this experience?

2. Describe a world where the first are last and the last are first. Where do you fit in this world? Where do you want to fit?

3. Recall a time when you saw God's kingdom being lived out. How did you recognise God's kingdom? How did you respond to this experience? Were you part of the kingdom? Did you join in once you recognised God's kingdom being lived out?

4. What does it mean to you to live a life of service? What kinds of actions are required? Who do you know who lives a life of service?

5. Does living a life of service mean giving up material possessions and social status? Why or why not?

Wednesday 20 November

1. Recall a time when you have been estranged from a friend or family member. What emotions did you feel during that time? How did you react to this experience? Was it difficult to continue loving the estranged person? How was the relationship restored—or severed?

2. To whom might you write a letter of love? What might you say in your letter? What does this person need to hear from you?

3. Gerald McCann describes the Bible as God's love letter to us. Is this how you experience scripture? If not, what is your experience with the Bible? How do you view its teachings?

4. Describe a time when you felt God's deep love for you. What were the circumstances? How did you become aware of God's love during that time? How did you respond to his love?

5. What are your favourite passages of scripture? Would you describe them as parts of a love letter? What do your favourite passages tell you about your relationship with God?

6. How do you engage with the Bible? How does your church community encourage or support your study of scripture? How could you help others to make Bible study a central part of their lives?

Wednesday 27 November

1. Is it easy or hard for you to express gratitude in your daily life? Why? What practices would help you to express your gratitude more freely?

2. Describe a time when you felt very grateful. Why were you grateful? How did you express your gratitude? How did expressing gratitude make you feel?

3. Who in your life is particularly good at expressing gratitude? What do you admire about this person? How does their gratitude affect the people around them?

4. Have you ever prayed using the alphabet as a structure? What did you like and dislike about this practice? What other methods have you used to structure your prayer time?

5. Read Psalm 118:19–29. What are some of the reasons the psalmist states for giving thanks to God? Which of these reasons is most important for you? Why do you give thanks to God?

6. What do you think about the practice of looking for things to be grateful about when you are feeling grumpy? Do you think this practice might help to balance the grumpiness with gratitude?

Wednesday 4 December

1. What type of music do you most enjoy? Describe a time when music was an important part of your spiritual life. How does music help you to engage with God and with your faith?

2. When have you felt most 'in tune' with the people in your community? What helped you to feel this way? Did this feeling continue?

3. Recall a time when you were part of a diverse group of people. What types of diversity were present? How did you feel in this setting? Did that diversity result in tension—or harmony? What did you learn from this experience?

4. Read 1 Corinthians 12:4-11. What spiritual gifts have you been given? How do you use your gifts in your daily life?

5. What spiritual practices or disciplines help you to feel spiritually 'in tune' with God? What new spiritual practice would you like to try in order to deepen your relationship with God?

Wednesday 11 December

1. Do you have a regular prayer routine? Do you pray in a particular place or at a particular time each day? How would having a prayer routine be helpful?

2. Do you prefer to pray alone or with others? Why is praying with others helpful or meaningful to you?

3. Why do you pray? What encourages you to keep praying even when it is difficult?

4. What are some of your favourite prayer forms or methods? How do you use these in your personal prayer practice?

5. Describe a time when you experienced the power of prayer. What did you or others pray for at that time? What convinced you that prayer was important? What was special about that prayer?

Wednesday 18 December

1. Recall a time when you were fearful of trying something new. What did you fear? How did you deal with your fears? Who or what encouraged you at this time?

2. In Exodus 3—4 Moses makes excuses to avoid being God's messenger to the Israelites, but God persists and empowers Moses to be a messenger. What excuses do you make when you would rather not follow God's call to service? How have others responded to your excuses? How has God responded?

3. What types of service opportunities do you most enjoy? Why? What types of service opportunities make you the most fearful or uncomfortable? Why?

4. Name some ways you have served your community in the past year. Which of these were the most meaningful to you? Which taught you the most about yourself and God?

5. What service opportunities would you like to encourage your church to follow up during the coming year? Name some local mission projects and brainstorm with your group about ways to become involved.

6. Is it important to always say 'yes' when you are asked to serve? How do you know when to say 'no'?

Wednesday 25 December

1. How do you and your family remember to focus on Jesus during the season of Advent and on Christmas Day? What are some new and different ways you might encourage yourself and others to reflect on the importance of Jesus during this season?

2. Describe a Christmas when you felt close to God. What helped you to feel this way? What traditions, experiences or people helped you to feel God's presence?

3. If someone asked you to explain the importance of Jesus for your life and for the world, what would you say? What aspects of Jesus' life, teachings or being would you emphasise as most important?

4. Troy suggests: 'Jesus is the window through which we see God.' How do you respond to this statement? Do you agree or disagree? Share an experience that illustrates your response.

5. What does it mean to you that God chose to become human in the person of Jesus? Is this important for you? Why or why not?

6. Is Jesus the only window through which you see God? What are some other 'windows' that you have experienced?

Journal page

Creating Community

Ancient ways for modern churches

Simon Reed

There is much talk today of 'new ways of being church' and 'new monastic spirituality'. As Simon Reed explored the Celtic roots of the Christian faith, in community with others who drew inspiration from our spiritual ancestors in the British Isles, he came to realise that the third-millennium church has much in common with the first-millennium church and, more importantly, much to learn from it.

In *Creating Community*, he introduces us to a new but at the same time very old way of being church which is based upon three core elements: a Way of Life, a network of Soul Friends, and a rhythm of prayer. The book shows how the rediscovery of these elements by Christians today offers a vital key that opens up an ancient way for modern churches, one that not only helps to bring believers to lasting maturity but creates genuine and much-needed community in an increasingly fragmented world.

ISBN 978 0 85746 009 7   £7.99
To order a copy of this book, please turn to the order form on page 159.

Also available for Kindle.

Real God in the Real World

Advent and Christmas readings on the coming of Christ

Trystan Owain Hughes

This book (the BRF Advent book for 2013) offers a lively, engaging and accessible look at the theme of the Incarnation, the mysterious event at the heart of Christmas, using personal stories, illustrations from popular culture and the arts, as well as daily Bible readings. The starting point is what the 'Word made flesh' means for us and how the first Christmas should still have an impact on our everyday lives.

We will be taken on an absorbing journey to help us recognise the person of Jesus in the people we meet, the conversations we have, and even in our relationship with nature and the arts. By the end of our journey, we will not only recognise Christ in others but also in ourselves, as we model ourselves on him and share his love, compassion and peace with our neighbours, whoever they are and whatever their backgrounds.

ISBN 978 0 85746 265 7   £7.99

To order a copy of this book, please turn to the order form on page 159.

Also available for Kindle.

Travellers of the Heart

Exploring new pathways on our spiritual journey

Michael Mitton

In this book, one of the UK's leading authors on Christian spirituality and personal renewal shares his own faith journey, in the context of exploring some of the different spiritual traditions that have influenced Christian witness over the past 40 or so years.

Building on themes in his previous book, *Dreaming of Home*, Michael Mitton explores how encompassing something of the breadth of Christian spirituality, from Charismatic to Catholic, via Celtic, can not only enrich our faith but strengthen the mission of the Church: 'I have chosen to start with my own experience, not because I am any kind of expert but because the best tutors to me over the years have been those prepared to share with me their stories, their ups and downs of life, their struggles and discoveries. Often their experiences have been very different from my own, but as I listen to them, they help me reflect on what is taking place in me.'

ISBN 978 0 85746 221 3   £7.99

To order a copy of this book, please turn to the order form on page 159.

Also available for Kindle.

I'm Fine

Removing masks and growing into wholeness

Wendy Billington

Wendy Billington gently explores ways of helping people remove the 'I'm fine!' mask and grow through the challenges posed by issues such as loneliness, low self-esteem and parenting pain, as well as a variety of addictive behaviours. Those struggling with particular problems in their lives may feel they can't be honest about their circumstances even—perhaps especially—in a church context. Isolation, shame, and anxiety about how others will perceive them can add to their difficulties, compounding them with a sense of being locked in with the problem.

Using case studies, Bible teaching and practical guidelines, Wendy shows how church members can understand and support one another, not only helping individuals but building a community that is characterised by loving, sensitive pastoral care.

ISBN 978 1 84101 871 3 £6.99
To order a copy of this book, please turn to the order form on page 159.

Also available for Kindle.

Bible Reading Resources Pack

Thank you for reading BRF Bible reading notes. BRF has been producing a variety of Bible reading notes for over 90 years, helping people all over the UK and the world connect with the Bible on a personal level every day.

Could you help us find other people who would enjoy our notes?

We produce a Bible Reading Resource Pack for church groups to use to encourage regular Bible reading.

This FREE pack contains:

- Samples of all BRF Bible reading notes.
- Our Resources for Personal Bible Reading catalogue, providing all you need to know about our Bible reading notes.
- A ready-to-use church magazine feature about BRF notes.
- Ready-made sermon and all-age service ideas to help your church into the Bible (ideal for Bible Sunday events).
- And much more!

How to order your FREE pack:

- Visit: www.biblereadingnotes.org.uk/request-a-bible-reading-resources-pack/
- Telephone: 01865 319700
- Post: Complete the form below and post to: Bible Reading Resource Pack, BRF, 15 The Chambers, Vineyard, Abingdon, OX14 3FE

Name...

Address ....

....Postcode...

Telephone ....

Email..

Please send me...............................Bible Reading Resources Pack(s).

This pack is produced free of charge for all UK addresses but, if you wish to offer a donation towards our costs, this would be appreciated. If you require a pack to be sent outside of the UK, please contact us for details of postage and packing charges. Tel: +44 1865 319700. Thank you.

BRF is a Registered Charity

Subscriptions

The Upper Room is published in January, May and September.

Individual subscriptions

The subscription rate for orders for 4 or fewer copies includes postage and packing: THE UPPER ROOM annual individual subscription   £14.10

Church subscriptions

Orders for 5 copies or more, sent to ONE address, are post free:
THE UPPER ROOM annual church subscription   £11.10

Please do not send payment with order for a church subscription. We will send an invoice with your first order.

Please note that the annual billing period for church subscriptions runs from 1 May to 30 April.

Copies of the notes may also be obtained from Christian bookshops.

Single copies of *The Upper Room* will cost £3.70. Prices valid until 30 April 2014.

Giant print version

The Upper Room is available in giant print for the visually impaired, from:

Torch Trust for the Blind
Torch House
Torch Way,
Northampton Road
Market Harborough
LE16 9HL

Tel: 01858 438260
www.torchtrust.org

Individual Subscriptions

☐ I would like to take out a subscription myself (complete your name and address details only once)

☐ I would like to give a gift subscription (please complete both name and address sections below)

Your name...

Your address..

....Postcode......................................

Your telephone number..

Gift subscription name...

Gift subscription address..

....Postcode......................................

Gift message (20 words max)...

....

Please send *The Upper Room* beginning with the January 2014 / May 2014 / September 2014 issue: (delete as applicable)

THE UPPER ROOM ☐ £14.10

Please complete the payment details below and send, with appropriate payment, to: BRF, 15 The Chambers, Vineyard, Abingdon OX14 3FE

Total enclosed £.......... (cheques should be made payable to 'BRF')

Payment by ☐ cheque ☐ postal order ☐ Visa ☐ Mastercard ☐ Switch

Card no: | | | | | | | | | | | | | | | | | | | | |

Expires: | | | | | Security code: | | | |

Issue no (Switch): | | | | |

Signature (essential if paying by credit/Switch card) ....

☐ Please do not send me further information about BRF publications

☐ Please send me a Bible reading resources pack to encourage Bible reading in my church

BRF is a Registered Charity

Church Subscriptions

☐ Please send me ... copies of *The Upper Room* January 2014 / May 2014 / September 2014 issue (delete as applicable)

Name..

Address ....

....Postcode...................................

Telephone ....

Email...

Please send this completed form to:
BRF, 15 The Chambers, Vineyard, Abingdon OX14 3FE

Please do not send payment with this order. We will send an invoice with your first order.

Christian bookshops: All good Christian bookshops stock BRF publications. For your nearest stockist, please contact BRF.

Telephone: The BRF office is open between 09.15 and 17.30. To place your order, telephone 01865 319700; fax 01865 319701.

Web: Visit www.brf.org.uk

☐ Please send me a Bible reading resources pack to encourage Bible reading in my church

BRF is a Registered Charity